I0502758

TABLE OF CONTENTS

EXECUTIVE SUMMARY

The role of various forms of third party assistance in tax return preparation in the United States has become increasingly important. For 2007 and 2008, over 80 percent of all federal individual income tax returns were prepared by paid tax return preparers or by taxpayers using consumer tax preparation software.[1] The IRS acknowledged this trend with the inclusion of the following objectives in its strategic plan: 1) Strengthen partnerships with tax practitioners, tax return preparers, and other third parties in order to ensure effective tax administration; and 2) Ensure that all tax practitioners, tax return preparers, and other third parties in the tax system adhere to professional standards and follow the law.[2] In June 2009, IRS Commissioner Douglas Shulman launched the Return Preparer Review to help accomplish these objectives.

The IRS sought to have its review process be an open and transparent discussion of the issues with the tax return preparer community, the associated industry, consumer advocacy groups, and the American public. The IRS solicited input from a diverse community of stakeholders through multiple outlets. The IRS thanks the hundreds of individuals and organizations who took part in this review and looks forward to a continuing productive relationship to implement the recommendations in this report.

A. Tax Return Preparer Industry

Currently, any person may prepare a federal tax return for any other person for a fee. All tax return preparers are subject to some oversight, but the level of oversight depends on whether the tax return preparer holds a professional license, has been enrolled to practice before the IRS, chooses to file returns electronically and the jurisdiction where he or she prepares returns.

The precise number of tax return preparers is not known, but the IRS estimates that there are between 900,000 and 1.2 million individuals preparing tax returns for a fee.[3] Although some tax return preparers (*e.g.*, attorneys and certified public accountants) are licensed by their States and others are enrolled to practice by the IRS, a large share of tax return preparers do not pass any government or professionally mandated competency requirements before they prepare a federal tax return.

All paid tax return preparers are subject to civil penalties for actions ranging from knowingly preparing a return that understates the taxpayer's liability to failing to sign or provide an identification number on a return they prepare. Tax return preparers who demonstrate a pattern of misconduct may be enjoined from preparing further returns. Additionally, the IRS may pursue and impose criminal penalties against a tax return preparer for the most severe misconduct.

---

[1] Internal Revenue Service Office of Research.

[2] 2009-2013 IRS Strategic Plan (April 2009), http://www.irs.gov/pub/irs-pdf/p3744.pdf.

[3] IRS Office of Program Evaluation and Risk Analysis, *Paid Preparer Review for National Public Liaison* (Sept. 2007).

Attorneys, certified public accountants, enrolled agents and other individuals authorized to practice before the IRS who prepare returns are subject to additional Federal oversight. Collectively known as *Practitioners*, these individuals must adhere to the more stringent standards of practice promulgated in Part 10 of Title 31 of the Code of Federal Regulations and reprinted in Treasury Department Circular 230. Practitioners who violate these standards of practice or who are shown to be incompetent or disreputable may be censured, suspended or disbarred from practice. The IRS Office of Professional Responsibility is charged with investigating allegations of Practitioner misconduct and conducting disciplinary proceedings, where warranted.

B. Stakeholder and Public Input

Through the public comment process, commenters overwhelmingly expressed support for efforts to increase the oversight of paid tax return preparers, particularly for those who are not attorneys, certified public accountants, or other individuals authorized to practice before the IRS. Highlights from an IRS analysis of the responses include:

- 98 percent of the individuals who offered comments on oversight and enforcement for paid tax return preparers favor increased efforts;
- 88 percent of the individuals who expressed an opinion on registering paid tax return preparers favor registration;
- 90 percent of the individuals who commented on education and testing favor minimum education or testing requirements for paid tax return preparers;
- 98 percent of the individuals who commented on quality and ethics favor establishment of quality and ethics standards for paid tax return preparers;
- 99 percent of the individuals who provided comments on outreach and communication for paid tax return preparers favor increased efforts.

Additionally, several commenters expressed concerns about the consumer and commercial tax preparation software industry. The number of tax return preparers and taxpayers who rely on tax preparation software to assist them in the preparation of federal tax returns grows each year.

Many commenters raised concerns about the availability and use of refund settlement products (*e.g.*, refund anticipation loans and refund anticipation checks/cards) through tax return preparers. These commenters questioned whether the purchasers of these products understand the full costs and obligations of the products.

C. Recommendations

After consideration of the input provided through the public comment process, the IRS believes that taxpayers, tax administration and the tax professional industry and related service providers will be better served through the implementation of a number of changes in how the industry participants are overseen. The recommended changes, which can be achieved through the issuance of regulations, are:

I.   Mandatory Tax Return Preparer Registration

- The IRS will require all individuals who are required to sign a federal tax return as a paid tax return preparer to register and obtain a preparer tax identification number. The IRS may charge a reasonable, nonrefundable fee to register as a tax return preparer. The preparer tax identification number will be the exclusive number used to identify any tax return preparer submitting returns to the IRS;
- The IRS will study the impact and necessity of expanding this registration requirement to nonsigning tax return preparers in the future;
- The IRS will make tax return preparer registration effective for three-year periods and require tax return preparers to renew their registration every three years.

II.   Competency Examination Requirement

- The IRS will establish competency testing for all paid tax return preparers required to register with the IRS who are not attorneys, certified public accountants or enrolled agents;
- The IRS will assess the quality of return preparation by those exempted from testing (*e.g.* attorneys, certified public accountants, enrolled agents) to determine whether there is a need to expand competency testing to include these individuals in the future;
- The IRS will perform suitability checks on those paid tax return preparers required to complete competency testing;
- There will not be any "grandfathering" from these testing requirements based upon past tax return preparation experience;
- Initially, the IRS will offer two competency examinations: One examination will cover wage and nonbusiness income Form 1040 series returns; another examination will cover wage and small business income Form 1040 series returns;
- The IRS plans to add a third test to address the competency of the tax return preparer with regard to business tax rules after the three-year implementation phase is completed;
- The IRS will develop transition rules to avoid significant interruption of services to taxpayers during the initial testing period. The preliminary approach will require that competency testing requirements be met no later than the required renewal date for tax return preparer registration.

III.   Continuing Professional Education

- The IRS will require 15 hours of annual continuing professional education, including three hours of federal tax law updates, two hours of tax preparer ethics and 10 hours of federal tax law topics, for tax return preparers who are required to register;

- The continuing professional education requirements will not apply to attorneys, certified public accountants, enrolled agents or others enrolled to practice before the IRS because these individuals generally must complete continuing education requirements to retain their professional credentials;
- The IRS will assess the quality of return preparation by those exempted from continuing professional education (*e.g.* attorneys, certified public accountants, enrolled agents and others enrolled to practice before the IRS) to determine whether there is a need to expand continuing professional education to include these individuals in the future;
- The IRS will reach out to the various licensing authorities for attorneys, certified public accountants and other tax professionals to encourage them to support annual continuing professional education that includes federal tax law topics and updates and ethics for those individuals who are licensed by them and who prepare federal tax returns;
- Tax return preparers will be required to self-certify the completion of continuing professional education at the time of registration renewal. The IRS will perform random checks to verify compliance.

IV.   Ethical Standards

- The IRS will place all signing and nonsigning tax return preparers under Treasury Department Circular 230. The authority granted to those individuals who do not have professional licenses and who are not enrolled agents, enrolled actuaries or enrolled retirement plan agents will be limited to preparing tax returns and representing their clients as currently permitted during an examination of any return prepared by the tax return preparer.

V.   Tax Return Preparer Enforcement

- The IRS will implement a comprehensive enforcement strategy that includes applying significant examination and collection resources to tax return preparer compliance;
- The IRS will study how to enhance the effectiveness of traditional enforcement tools and incorporate new non-traditional enforcement tools (*e.g.*, directed notices and preparer visits) into the enforcement activities directed at tax return preparers;
- The IRS will study the impact an enhanced return preparer enforcement strategy has on taxpayer compliance and consider further changes to the IRS enforcement strategy dependent on the outcomes realized;
- The IRS will increase the coordination among its operating divisions and increase the staffing of the Office of Professional Responsibility to allow for increased investigations of practitioner, including tax return preparer misconduct.

VI.   Tax Return Preparation Software

- The IRS will establish a task force that will seek the input of the tax preparation software industry, state government representatives, and other relevant stakeholders to address identified risks associated with the dependence of tax administration on consumer and commercial tax preparation software, and discuss the possibility of establishing industry standards.

VII.   Refund Settlement Products

- The IRS will convene a working group to review the refund settlement product industry. Part of this review will include analyzing opportunities to improve refund delivery options.
- The IRS will assess the effectiveness of its provision of the debt indicator on reduction of costs and improvements in service to taxpayers;

VIII.   Public Awareness and Service Enhancements

- The IRS will develop a public awareness campaign to educate taxpayers, paid tax return preparers, and IRS employees about the new standards and requirements for tax return preparers;
- The IRS will develop a searchable database of tax return preparers who have registered and passed the competency examination.

INTRODUCTION

Over the past twenty years, there has been a significant shift in the way that U.S. taxpayers complete and file their tax returns. Increased use of paid tax return preparers as well as explosive growth in the use of technology by both self-preparers and tax professionals has altered the ways in which tax filing is accomplished. At the same time, for many U.S. taxpayers, the interactions relating to tax filing represents one of the biggest financial transactions they undertake each year. More than ever, taxpayers are relying on tax return preparers and consumer tax return preparation software to help them prepare their returns.

In addition to preparing tax returns, tax return preparers have an opportunity to educate taxpayers about the tax laws, facilitate electronic filing, and reduce the stress and anxiety often associated with the tax filing season.   Tax return preparers may explain to the taxpayer his or her rights and responsibilities. Tax return preparers advise their client taxpayers, identifying issues where the guidance is unclear and assessing the risks associated with a possible reporting position. A well-educated and competent tax return preparer can prevent inadvertent errors, possibly saving the taxpayer from unwanted problems later and the IRS from consuming valuable compliance resources.

Recent studies conducted by the Government Accountability Office, the Treasury Inspector General for Tax Administration, and others suggest, however, that our system of federal tax administration and a large number of taxpayers may be poorly served by some tax return preparers. Although GAO and TIGTA could not estimate the number of taxpayers adversely affected, they reported that returns completed by some tax return preparers were inaccurate. In some cases, they found that the tax return preparer failed to perform sufficient due diligence or took positions that the tax return preparer knew were not supportable.

While the IRS has encouraged taxpayers to take some common sense steps in choosing a tax return preparer, more concrete steps are necessary. In June 2009, the Internal Revenue Service launched a Tax Return Preparer Review. As part of this effort, the IRS received input from a large and diverse community, including tax return preparers, tax professional organizations, members of associated industries, federal and state government officials, consumer groups and the public. The findings and recommendations of this review, which are outlined in this report, are intended to better leverage the tax return preparer community with the twin goals of increasing taxpayer compliance and ensuring uniform and high ethical standards of conduct for tax return preparers.

HISTORY OF THE U.S. TAX RETURN PREPARATION INDUSTRY

Commercial tax return preparation began primarily as an ancillary service for those in the accounting, auditing, bookkeeping or legal industries. Tax return preparation was considered an extension of the services that businesses within those industries were providing their clients. Many of the businesses that provided tax return preparation services to their clients in the first part of the 20th century did so as a courtesy for little or no charge. Most individual taxpayers who were required to pay income taxes and file returns[4] during this time either prepared their own returns or had their returns prepared by their local IRS office.

By the end of World War II, most Americans had an income tax obligation.[5] The number of persons affected by the federal income tax after the war increased the importance of tax return preparation services. Most taxpayers could no longer walk into their local IRS office and have their return prepared by the early 1960s. Tax return preparation was no longer an ancillary service for the accounting, auditing bookkeeping and legal services industries, although many in those fields continue to provide return preparation services.

---

[4] Less than six percent of Americans had an income tax obligation as late as 1939.
[5] More than 75 percent of the American population had an income tax obligation by the end of World War II.

Today, the tax return preparation industry has its own standard industry classification.[6] It is a multibillion dollar industry with several thousand commercial tax return preparation businesses open across the United States and around the world. The largest of these businesses has thousands of locations, while the smallest businesses may operate out of rented kiosk space in a local shopping mall or from the proprietor's residence. Many tax return preparers operate year round; others may operate only during a portion of the first four months of the calendar year. Although some tax return preparers limit their business to preparation of tax returns, others offer their own ancillary services, including tax return preparation software and refund settlement products.

CURRENT TAX RETURN PREPARER ENVIRONMENT

Today, a majority of U.S. taxpayers rely on tax return preparers to assist them in meeting their federal tax filing obligations. Between 1993 and 2005, the number of taxpayers who prepared their own tax returns without outside assistance fell more than two-thirds (Figure 1). For 2007 and 2008, over 80 percent of all federal tax returns were filed either using a tax return preparer or software. Specifically, approximately 87 million federal individual income tax returns were prepared by paid tax return preparers.[7] Additionally, the IRS is projecting an increase in these numbers for 2009.

---

[6] United States Census Bureau, *North American Industry Classification System* (2007).
[7] Internal Revenue Service Office of Research.

Figure 1

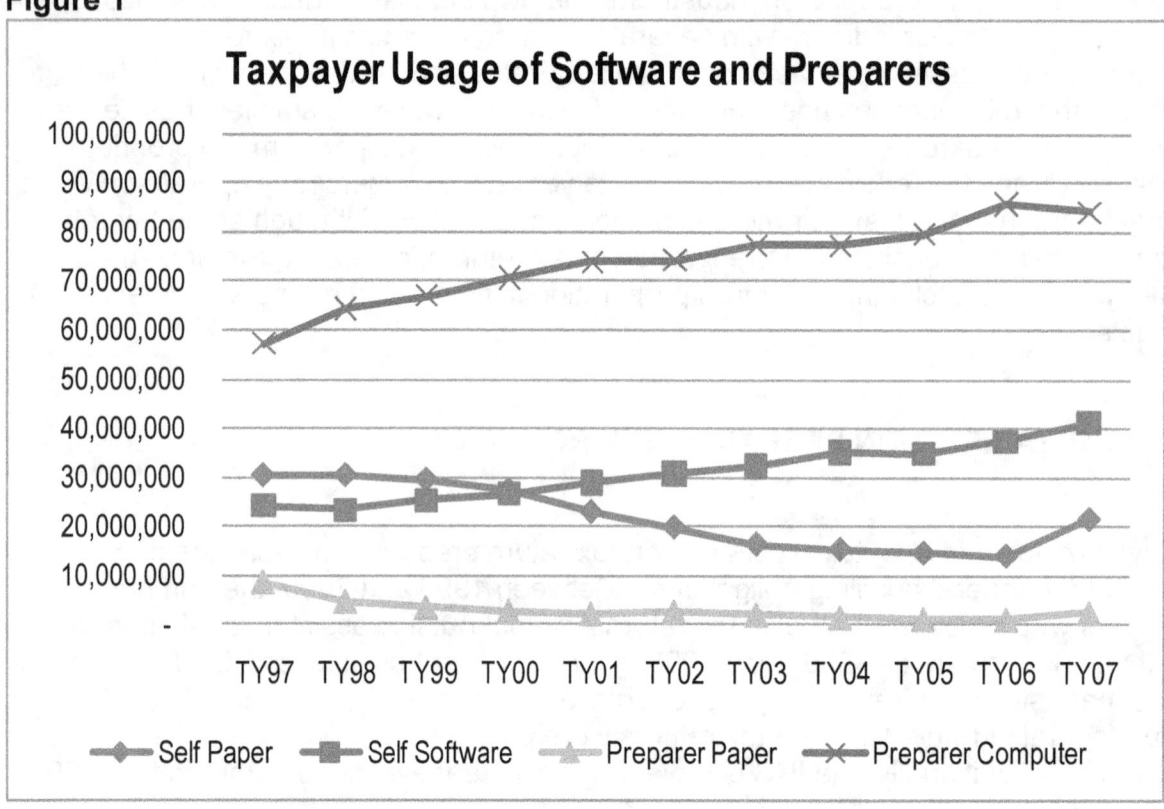

Currently, any person may prepare a federal tax return for any other person for a fee. Due to the lack of registration and inconsistent reporting, the number of tax return preparers is not known. The IRS estimates that there are between 900,000 and 1.2 million paid tax return preparers currently (Figure 2).[8] Although some tax return preparers (*e.g.*, attorneys and certified public accountants) are licensed by their states and others are enrolled to practice by the IRS, many tax return preparers do not pass any competency requirements before they prepare a federal tax return. This last category of tax return preparer is not required to have any minimum education, knowledge, training or skill before they prepare a tax return for a fee.

---

[8] IRS Office of Program Evaluation and Risk Analysis, *Paid Preparer Review for National Public Liaison* (Sept. 2007).

Figure 2

Return Preparers	Estimated Population	Number of Returns Prepared
Estimated Overall Return Preparer Totals	0.9 – 1.2 million	86.6 million
Enrolled Agents	42,896 active	Unknown
Certified Public Accountants	646,520 as of 2006	Unknown
Attorneys	1,180,386	Unknown
Enrolled Retirement Plan Agents	123	Unknown
Unenrolled Return Preparers	Unknown	Unknown
Volunteers	82,653 volunteers	3.02 million

Recent studies show that 94 percent of taxpayers who use tax return preparers generally follow their advice.[9] Sixty-two percent of taxpayers said they follow their tax return preparer's advice all the time.[10] With tax return preparers preparing almost 60 percent of all returns filed, their impact on tax administration is significant.

A.   Tax Return Preparation Software

The consumer and commercial tax software industry is one of the largest and fastest growing industries associated with tax return preparation. Taxpayers self-prepared and electronically filed 32 million tax returns using consumer tax preparation software during the 2009 filing season.[11] These taxpayers rely on tax software to answer their tax law questions and to assist them in the preparation of accurate returns. Thus, for these taxpayers, the consumer tax preparation software is a low cost alternative to hiring a paid tax return preparer or to preparing tax returns manually on their own.

Professional tax return preparers also use commercial tax preparation software to prepare and electronically file returns for their clients. During the 2009 filing season, tax return preparers used tax preparation software to prepare 61.8 million tax returns.[12]

Despite large volumes of returns prepared using consumer and commercial tax preparation software, quality control over these products rests exclusively with the

---

[9] IRS, *AES2 Taxpayer Survey, Question 13* (2009); IRS, *Taxpayer Assistance Blueprint, Phase 2* (2007); Barr, Dokko, *Tax Filing Experiences and Withholding Preferences of Low- and Moderate-Income Households: Preliminary Evidence from a New Survey* (2006).
[10] Id.
[11] Electronic Tax Administration Research and Analysis System, *IMF Electronic Transmitted Returns* (2009).
[12] Electronic Tax Administration Research and Analysis System, *IMF Electronic Transmitted Returns and Modernized Electronic Filed BMF Returns* (2009).

software publishers. There are approximately 80 tax preparation software packages available for purchase in the U.S. currently.[13] About half of those packages are intended for taxpayers who intend to self prepare their tax returns (consumer software) and about half are intended for use by professional tax return preparers (commercial software).[14] While the number of tax software providers appears robust, four companies dominate the market, accounting for 80 percent of the tax returns filed electronically over the last two years.[15]

Currently, vendors develop tax preparation software complying with instructions provided by the IRS in documents such as Publication 1346, Electronic Return File Specifications for Individual Income Tax Returns. These software packages are tested by the IRS for transmission suitability (*i.e.* does the software interact appropriately with IRS systems to enable the electronic filing of the return). There is, however, no direct evaluation of software packages for accuracy or usability. Further, although the IRS can impose penalties on tax preparation software companies for unauthorized disclosure or use of a taxpayer's personal and tax-related information, little is known about the security and privacy of taxpayer information held by the companies.

B.   Refund Settlement Products

An estimated 20.5 million taxpayers purchase ancillary products that provide them quicker access to the amount of their expected tax refunds.[16] The two primary products are Refund Anticipation Loans (RALs) and Refund Anticipation Checks/Cards (RACs). RALs are short-term loans from a financial institution secured by the taxpayer's expected refund. Several tax preparation companies and tax return preparers facilitate and advertise RALs to taxpayers, although the taxpayer contracts with the financial institution — not the tax return preparer — as lender for the loan. The lender may require the taxpayer to sign a consent form for the IRS' Debt Indicator Program[17] when the taxpayer applies for the RAL. The lender uses the Debt Indicator to assist in its evaluation of the taxpayer's application for the RAL. The taxpayer generally receives the funds, less fees, within a day of applying for the loan. The loan is repaid when the refund is sent by the IRS to a bank account specified by the lender.

RACs are non-loan alternatives to RALs. With a RAC, the financial institution establishes a temporary account for the taxpayer to receive his or her refund. When the tax refund is deposited, the taxpayer is given a check or a debit card for the refund amount, less fees. RACs are used to expedite refunds for taxpayers who do not have bank accounts and would otherwise have to wait for a paper check or for taxpayers who

---

[13] Id.

[14] Id.

[15] Id.

[16] IRS Electronic Tax Administration, *Compliance Data Warehouse* (2007, updated fall 2009).

[17] Through the Debt Indicator Program, a taxpayer or an authorized third-party is advised whether the taxpayer has any outstanding debts collectible by the Federal government that will be offset as all or a portion of the taxpayer's refund. A negative Debt Indicator result does not, however, guarantee that the refund will be paid.

do not have available funds to pay the fees for tax return preparation prior to receiving the refund (or both).

Use of these refund settlement products has been increasing over time (Figure 3). Between 2001 and 2007, the number of taxpayers using these products grew from 15 million to approximately 20.5 million (or from 11 percent of individual income tax returns to nearly 14 percent).[18]

Figure 3: Taxpayers' Requests for Bank Products for Tax Years 2005 – 2007

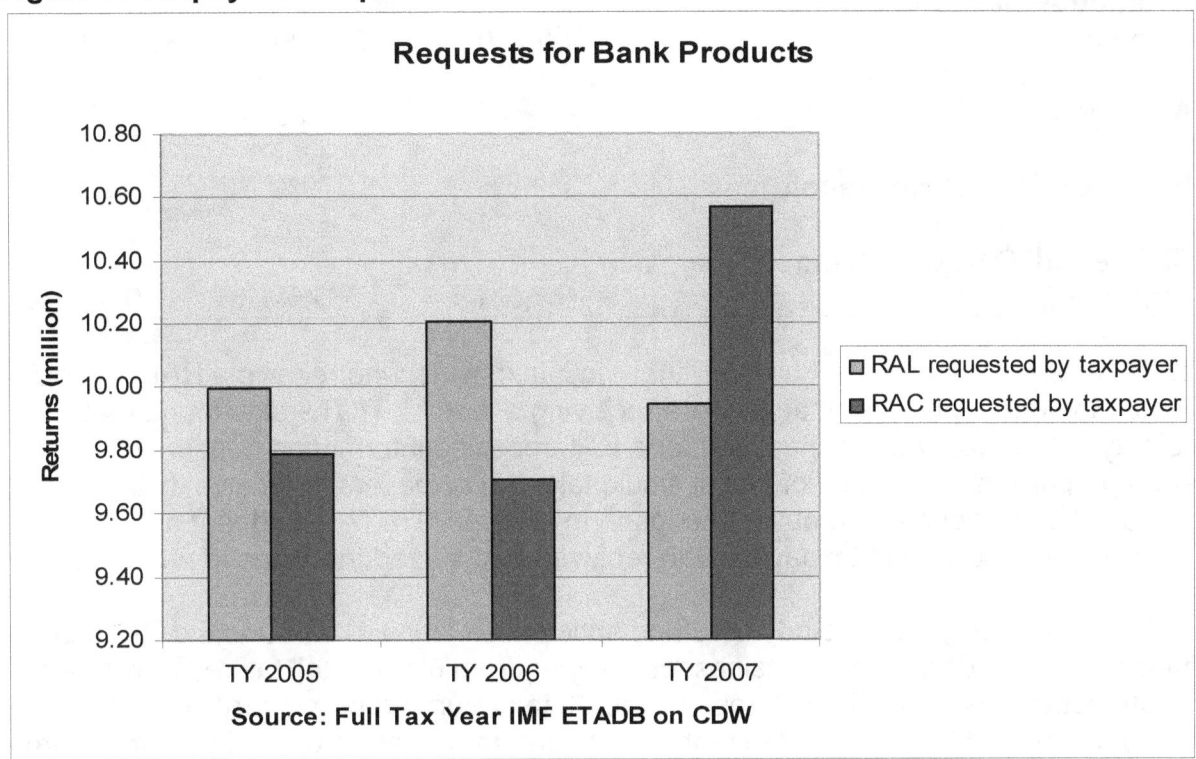

Taxpayers who use RALs and RACs have an average income considerably lower than that of other taxpayers (Figure 4) and have a significantly higher incidence of receiving the earned income tax credit. Consumer and taxpayer advocacy groups suggest that taxpayers who purchase these products may not comprehend the true, high costs of the product.[19] Fees for RALs vary widely. In a recent GAO study, the annual percentage rates for the loans in the study ranged from 36 percent to over 500 percent.[20] And while RALs are subject to Truth in Lending Act Requirements, GAO found that tax return preparers in their study did not use consistent methods to calculate rates presented in advertisements.[21] Recent research by TIGTA supports the argument that tax return

---

[18] IRS Electronic Tax Administration, *Compliance Data Warehouse* (2007, updated fall 2009).
[19] General Accountability Office, *Refund Anticipation Loans*, GAO-08-800R (June 5, 2008).
[20] Id.
[21] Id.

preparers do not provide many RAL applicants with a complete understanding of the full costs of these products.[22]

Figure 4: Taxpayer Characteristics by Bank Product Type for Tax Year 2004

	No Bank Product	RAL	RAC
Number of Returns (millions)	110.7	10.6	7.5
Average Adjusted Gross Income	$55,200	$22,400	$32,200
Average Age	45	35	36
Single or Head of Household	56%	79%	69%
Claimed EITC w/ Qualifying Children	7.5%	58.4%	40.4%

TIGTA's research suggests, however, that most taxpayers who receive a RAL are told by their tax return preparer that they are receiving a loan.[23] TIGTA also found that a majority of the taxpayers who applied for a RAL received information from their tax return preparer on the length of time it would take the taxpayers to receive their tax refund if they decided not to obtain the loan. In addition, TIGTA found that an overwhelming majority of taxpayers who received RALs used the loans to pay bills.

In 2008, GAO completed a study of refund anticipation loans.[24] GAO found RALs are marketed by a wide variety of businesses, ranging from major retail tax return preparers to automotive dealers to shoe stores. Of the 40 tax return preparers GAO called or visited, 37 offered RALs. Thirteen of the 40 tax return preparers offered year-round tax return preparation, while 27 were open only during the tax season and operated at tables or desks within businesses offering other products or services. Of the 27 tax return preparers open only during the tax season, 13 were located in businesses that GAO suggested targeted low-income customers (*e.g.*, check cashers, payday loan vendors, rent-to-own stores and pawn shops) and nine offered incentives to encourage customers to spend the refunds on the businesses' primary goods and services.

---

[22] Sixty-six percent of the 250 taxpayers who participated in a TIGTA survey after receiving RALS during the 2008 filing season stated that they were not provided with the annual interest rate for the loan. Treasury Inspector General for Tax Administration, *Many Taxpayers Who Obtain Refund Anticipation Loans Could Benefit From Free Tax Preparation Services*, TIGTA 2008-40-170 (August 29, 2008).

[23] Treasury Inspector General for Tax Administration, *Many Taxpayers Who Obtain Refund Anticipation Loans Could Benefit From Free Tax Preparation Services*, TIGTA 2008-40-170.

[24] Government Accountability Office, *Refund Anticipation Loans*, GAO-08-800R.

TAX RETURN PREPARER COMPLIANCE STUDIES

In 2006, the GAO conducted a review of the services offered by paid tax return preparers and the quality of the services rendered by these service providers.[25] As part of this review, GAO staff posed as taxpayers and "shopped" several outlets of chain commercial tax return preparation firms in a major metropolitan area. Two years later, the TIGTA conducted a similar review of unenrolled paid tax return preparers.[26] Although the size and non-representative aspects of the samples in these studies precluded GAO and TIGTA from generalizing their results and drawing conclusions about all paid tax return preparers, the results of these "shopping visits" are illuminating.

A. Government Accountability Office

The GAO study targeted 19 outlets of chain commercial tax return preparation firms.[27] The GAO staff asked tax return preparers at those 19 outlets to prepare federal tax returns under one of two scenarios for which staff from the GAO, Senate Committee on Finance and the Joint Committee on Taxation had previously completed tax returns and agreed upon the contents of the return and the correct amount of tax.

According to the GAO, only two of the 19 tax return preparers had the correct tax liability and refund amounts on the return they prepared and all 19 tax return preparers made a mistake on the prepared returns. Although most of the 19 tax return preparers included all income for which a payor had an information reporting requirement, three tax return preparers reported incorrect amounts of ordinary dividends or capital gain income. Eight of 19 tax return preparers reported the shopper's prior year's state tax refund incorrectly. Several tax return preparers did not ask about income from sources other than wages and, although all tax return preparers were told that there was income from casual self-employment arrangements, 10 of the 19 tax return preparers did not report this income as required. Several of the tax return preparers who did report this income on the returns they completed did not provide the shopper with correct information. One tax return preparer told the shopper that she did not have to report the income unless it was more than $3,200. Others advised that the shopper had discretion on whether to report this income because the IRS would not know about the income unless it was reported.

The tax return preparers also made mistakes when it came to claiming the proper amount of credits and deductions. For example, 10 shoppers were entitled to a credit for child care expenses for their shopper, but none of the tax return preparers who

---

[25] Government Accountability Office, *Paid Tax Return Preparers: In a limited Study, Chain Prepares Made Serious Errors*, GAO-06-563T (Apr. 4, 2006).

[26] Treasury Inspector General for Tax Administration, *Most Tax Returns Prepared by a Limited Sample of Unenrolled Preparers Contained Significant Errors*, Rept. # 2008-40-171 (Sept. 3, 2008).

[27] Government Accountability Office, *Paid Tax Return Preparers: In a limited Study, Chain Prepares Made Serious Errors*, GAO-06-563T.

prepared a return for these shoppers claimed the credit. Although nine shoppers would have benefitted by itemizing their deductions, two of the nine tax return preparers who prepared their returns only claimed the standard deduction. Of the seven tax return preparers who did itemize their shopper's deductions, five prepared returns claiming an incorrect amount of deductions. Six of these nine tax return preparers also erred in determining the amount of education credit to claim for the shopper. The 10 tax return preparers who were presented with an earned income tax credit scenario also made significant errors. Only one of these 10 tax return preparers asked all of the required questions and half of the 10 tax return preparers incorrectly reported that GAO's shopper was entitled to the earned income tax credit for two children when the shopper was only entitled to claim the credit for one of her children.

In addition to these computational errors, some tax return preparers did not include required identifying information. Four of the 19 tax return preparers did not sign the returns they prepared and two tax return preparers did not furnish their own identifying number. One tax return preparer did not include a company name and employer identification number.

B.   Treasury Inspector General for Tax Administration

The Treasury Inspector General for Tax Administration had its auditors pose as taxpayers and "shopped" 28 unenrolled tax return preparers[28] in a large metropolitan area for its study.[29] Of the 28 tax return preparers shopped by TIGTA, 12 were employed by outlets of chain commercial tax return preparation firms and 16 worked at, or owned, small, independent tax return preparation firms. The shopped tax return preparers were asked to prepare a federal tax return based on one of five scenarios developed by TIGTA. TIGTA did not consider any of the scenarios to be complex as the tax topics raised by each scenario were specific, straightforward, and not dependent on interpretation. Table 1 shows the various tax law topics covered in the five scenarios.

---

[28] The tax return preparers shopped by TIGTA were not attorneys, certified public accountants, enrolled agents, or enrolled actuaries.

[29] Treasury Inspector General for Tax Administration, *Most Tax Returns Prepared by a Limited Sample of Unenrolled Preparers Contained Significant Errors*, Rept. # 2008-40-171.

Table 1

Additional Child Tax Credit	Education Credits
Business Income and Expenses	Filing Status
Capital Gains	Income from Wages
Charitable Contributions	Individual Retirement Account Distribution
Child and Dependent Care	Interest Income
Child Tax Credit	Mortgage Interest Paid
Dependency Exemptions	Saver's Credit
Earned Income Tax Credit	Self-Employment Tax and Deduction

Each of the shopped tax return preparers used commercial tax preparation software to assist them in the preparation of the tax returns.

According to TIGTA, most of the 28 tax return preparers asked probing questions before and during the preparation of the tax returns and 16 of the 28 tax return preparers asked the shoppers to complete an information worksheet.[30] Tax return preparers who did not ask probing questions generally made assumptions or relied upon tax return preparation software to make eligibility determinations. The use of probing questions or an information worksheet was not an indication, however, of the accuracy of the resulting return. TIGTA found that 11 of the 16 tax return preparers who had the shopper complete a worksheet prepared an incorrect return. And, at least one tax return preparer who did not ask the shopper any probing questions nevertheless prepared a correct tax return.

Seven tax return preparers did not exercise due diligence when determining whether the shopper was eligible to receive the earned income tax credit. Although all seven tax return preparers completed the required Form 8867, *Paid Preparer's Earned Income Credit Checklist*, none asked any or all of the probing questions on the form. One tax return preparer complained to the shopper that the tax return preparation software prompts slowed down the preparation process.

Seventeen tax return preparers did not show the correct amount of tax owed or refund due on the returns they prepared.[31] Although all tax return preparers correctly reported income from savings account interest, wages, and self-employment, no tax return preparer correctly calculated the expenses relating to self-employment income.

---

[30] An information worksheet is a document tax return preparers use to gather names, social security numbers, sources of income received or earned, the length of time children who could be claimed as dependents lived in the home, and other information generally used in the preparation of a tax return.

[31] Id.

Figure 5: Results by Tax Law Topic

Topic	Correct	Incorrect	Percentage Correct
Additional Child Tax Credit (28 tax returns)	24	4	86%
Business Income (6 tax returns)	6	0	100%
Business Expenses (6 tax returns)	0	6	0%
Capital Gains (6 tax returns)	5	1	83%
Child and Dependent Care Credit (12 tax returns)	10	2	83%
Child Tax Credit (28 tax returns)	22	6	79%
Dependency Exemptions (28 tax returns)	26	2	93%
Earned Income Tax Credit (12 tax returns)	10	2	83%
Education Credits (12 tax returns)	6	6	50%
Filing Status (28 tax returns)	27	1	96%
Income – Wages (28 tax returns)	28	0	100%
Individual Retirement Account Distribution (17 tax returns)	15	2	88%
Interest Income (28 tax returns)	28	0	100%
Itemized deductions (5 tax returns)[1]	3	2	60%
Saver's Credit (23 tax returns)	18	5	78%
Self-Employment Tax and Deduction (12 tax returns)	1	11	8%

[1] *Itemized deduction tax law topic includes mortgage interest paid and charitable contributions.*

Source: Treasury Inspector General for Tax Administration, Most Tax Returns Prepared by a Limited Sample of Unenrolled Preparers Contained Significant Errors, *Rept. # 2008-40-171.*

If taxpayers had filed the 17 returns that did not show the correct amount of tax owed or refund due, the net effect would have been $12,828 in understated taxes.

TIGTA also found that the preparers of six of the 17 returns prepared incorrectly acted willfully or recklessly during the preparation of the shopped returns. These tax return preparers added or increased deductions without permission and, in some situations, did so after the shopper questioned whether they were entitled to receive the deductions. Examples include a tax return preparer who increased the child care expenses claimed on the return after the shopper explained to the tax return preparer that child care expenses were paid in cash and a tax return preparer who completed a return claiming a deduction for charitable contributions after the shopper stated that no charitable contributions were made. These six individuals prepared more than 950 tax returns during the 2008 filing season.

Additionally, a few of the shopped tax return preparers did not provide required identifying information. Five of the 28 tax return preparers did not sign the shopper's tax return as required, and two tax return preparers did not furnish their own identification numbers as required on the completed tax returns. Three tax return preparers did not protect their client's tax information from disclosure. These tax return preparers repeated their client's social security numbers aloud or had their client's return information visible on the computer screen or desk when other individuals were present in the office.

EXISTING OVERSIGHT OF TAX RETURN PREPARERS

All tax return preparers are subject to some oversight. The level of oversight depends on whether the tax return preparer holds a tax-related professional license, has been enrolled to practice before the IRS, and chooses to file returns electronically and on the jurisdictions in which they prepare returns. The different categories of tax return preparers are shown in Figure 6.

Figure 6 – Paid Tax Return Preparers

Attorneys	Certified Public Accountants	Enrolled Agents, Enrolled Actuaries and Enrolled Retirement Plan Agents	Unenrolled Tax Return Preparers
Members in good standing of the bar of the highest court of a state, territory, or possession of the United States.	Persons duly qualified to practice as a certified public accountant in any state, territory, or possession of the United States.	Professionals enrolled to practice before the IRS. Enrollment requires passing an examination or presenting evidence of qualifying experience.	Other tax return preparers who, except in a limited number of states, have no minimum education or training requirements.
Regulated by state licensing authorities and, if they practice before the IRS, under Treasury Department Circular 230*		Regulated by the IRS under Treasury Department Circular 230	Generally, not regulated

* The Regulations Governing the Practice of Attorneys, Certified Public Accountants, Enrolled Agents, Enrolled Actuaries, Enrolled Retirement Plan Agents and Appraisers before the Internal Revenue Service are published in 31 CFR Part 10 and reprinted in Treasury Department Circular 230

A.   Federal Regulation of Tax Return Preparers

All paid tax return preparers are subject to Internal Revenue Code penalties. Section 6694(a) of the Internal Revenue Code imposes a civil penalty on a tax return preparer who prepares a return that understates the taxpayer's liability where the understatement was due to a position that the tax return preparer knew or reasonably should have known was unreasonable. The penalty imposed on the tax return preparer is increased under section 6694(b) if the understatement is due to the tax return preparer's willful attempt to understate liability or reckless or intentional disregard for the rules. A tax return preparer may also be penalized for aiding or abetting in the understatement of a liability on a return under section 6701. Tax return preparers who demonstrate a pattern of misconduct may be enjoined from preparing further returns.

In addition, section 6695 imposes penalties on a tax return preparer who fails to perform certain acts. For example, a tax return preparer must sign the return and include his or her own identification number on the return. The tax return preparer must also provide the taxpayer with a copy of the return. The penalty for failing to meet these requirements is $50 per failure and cannot exceed $25,000 for each type of failure annually. These penalties generally will not be assessed if the tax return preparer shows that the violation was due to reasonable cause and not willful neglect.

Tax return preparers are also subject to criminal sanctions arising from improper conduct. For example, a tax return preparer that helps taxpayers prepare false or fraudulent returns may be liable and could receive a prison term and a fine of up to $100,000 under sections 7206 and 7207. Other penalties, both civil and criminal, prohibit tax return preparers from improperly disclosing or using the information taxpayers provide to a tax return preparer in connection with the preparation of a taxpayer's tax return. Civil and criminal penalties can be imposed for the same violation.

Attorneys, certified public accountants, enrolled agents and other individuals authorized to practice before the IRS who prepare returns are subject to additional federal oversight. Collectively known as *Practitioners*, these individuals must adhere to the more stringent standards of practice promulgated in Part 10 of Title 31 of the Code of Federal Regulations and reprinted in Treasury Department Circular 230. Practitioners who violate these standards of practice or who are shown to be incompetent or disreputable may be reprimanded, censured, suspended or disbarred from practice. The IRS Office of Professional Responsibility is charged with investigating allegations of practitioner misconduct and proposing appropriate disciplinary sanctions.

Additionally, the IRS, under its broad authority to regulate the filing of electronic returns, requires any tax return preparer who files returns electronically to comply with certain regulations. Under these regulations, the IRS may require the electronic return originator to pass background and credit history checks.

B. State Regulation of Tax Return Preparers

All states license attorneys and certified public accountants and four states have enacted legislation regulating return preparers generally. Oregon and California have been regulating return preparers since the 1970s. Maryland and New York have recently passed legislation and will begin regulating return preparers in the near future.

I. Oregon

Oregon requires individuals who prepare, advise or assist in the preparation of personal income tax returns for others for a fee to be licensed unless exempted.[32] Those

---

[32] OR. Rev. Stat. §673.615 (2009).

exempted from the licensing requirements include certified public accountants and public accountants licensed by the Oregon Board of Accountancy and members of the Oregon State Bar who prepare returns for their law clients.[33] Oregon also requires businesses that prepare tax returns to register.[34] All income tax preparation businesses must be operated by or employ a licensed tax consultant who provides services or who supervises tax preparers.

Oregon issues two types of licenses to individuals preparing income tax returns for a fee. Licensed Tax Consultants have the highest level of competency and may prepare returns as a self-employed tax practitioner or as a supervising tax practitioner. To become a licensed Tax Consultant, an individual must work as a tax preparer for a minimum of 780 hours during two of the last five years; complete a minimum of 15 hours of continuing education within one year of submitting an application; and pass Oregon's tax consultant examination.[35] Licensed Tax Preparers may lawfully prepare income tax returns under the supervision of a licensed Tax Consultant or other qualified person.[36] To become a licensed Tax Preparer, an individual must be at least 18 years of age; be a high school graduate or have passed an equivalency examination; complete a minimum of 80 hours of basic income tax law education; and pass Oregon's tax preparer examination.[37] Annually, licensees must complete a minimum of 30 hours of continuing education, maintain professional standards and state ethics, and file a license renewal form and pay appropriate fees.[38]

The Oregon Board of Tax Practitioners may refuse to issue or to renew a license, suspend or revoke a license, or reprimand a tax consultant or tax preparer on disciplinary grounds.[39] A licensee may be disciplined for negligence or incompetence in tax consultant practice or tax preparer practice; conviction of crimes involving dishonesty, fraud, or deception; conviction of willfully failing to pay taxes or file returns; conviction of willfully making false returns, or supplying false information, required under state or Federal tax laws; violation of the Board's code of professional conduct; and professional sanctions related to the practice of law or accountancy or to practice as an enrolled agent if the sanction was related to income tax preparation or if dishonesty, fraud, or deception was involved.[40] The Board also has the authority to assess civil penalties up to $5,000 and to order restitution to consumers harmed by tax preparation fraud.[41]

---

[33] OR. Rev. Stat. §673.610 (2009).
[34] OR. Rev. Stat. §673.643 (2009). The business registration is in addition to, and not in lieu of, the required registration for the individuals preparing, assisting in the preparation or advise other persons with respect to person income tax returns for a fee.
[35] OR. Rev. Stat. §673.625 (2009).
[36] OR. Rev. Stat. §673.615 (2009).
[37] OR. Rev. Stat. §673.625 (2009).
[38] OR. Rev. Stat. §673.655 (2009).
[39] OR. Rev. Stat. §673.700 (2009).
[40] Id.
[41] OR. Rev. Stat. §673.730(6) (2009).

II. California

California has been regulating return preparers since the 1970s.[42] California requires individuals who prepare or assist in the preparation of tax returns for a fee to register unless exempted.[43] Individuals exempted from this requirement include attorneys who are active members of the State Bar of California, certified public accountants who are licensed by the California Board of Accountancy, enrolled agents, and the employees of these categories of individuals.[44] To register, an individual must post a $5,000 surety bond and complete not less than 60 hours of instruction in basic personal income tax law education by an approved provider within the previous 18 months.[45] Registrants also must pay a registration fee of $25 and complete at least 20 hours of continuing education, including 12 hours in Federal taxation, 4 hours in California taxation, and additional 4 hours in either Federal or California taxation from an approved provider annually.[46]

III. Maryland

In 2008, the Maryland legislature passed, and the Governor signed, the Maryland Individual Tax Preparers Act.[47] This act provides that, effective June 1, 2010, any individual not otherwise exempted who offers individual income tax preparation services must be registered.[48] Individuals exempted from this registration requirement include certified public accountants licensed in Maryland or any other state; attorneys admitted to the practice of law in Maryland or any other state; individuals employed by a local or state government or by the Federal government, but only in performance of official duties; individuals enrolled to practice before the IRS who are governed under Circular 230; and an employee of, or assistant to, a licensed individual tax preparer, or exempted individual, in performance of duties on their behalf.[49] Although the registration requirement is effective on June 1, 2010, the Maryland Department of Labor, Licensing & Regulation has stated that the implementation of the Act is contingent on the appointment of the Board of Individual Tax Return Preparers and on the appropriation of funds.[50] To date, the Governor has not appointed a Board and the legislature has not appropriated funding.

---

[42] In 1997, the State legislature transferred responsibility for registering individuals as tax preparers; certifying the education of tax preparers; approving tax schools; and educating California taxpayers on the selection of tax professionals to The California Tax Education Council, a non-profit corporation.

[43] Cal. Bus. & Prof. Code §22253 (West 2009).

[44] Cal. Bus. & Prof. Code §22258 (West 2009).

[45] Cal. Bus. & Prof. Code §§22250 and 22255 (West 2009).

[46] Id.

[47] MD. CODE ANN., Bus. Occ. & Prof. §21-501 (West 2009).

[48] MD. CODE ANN., Bus. Occ. & Prof. §21-301 (West 2009).

[49] MD. CODE ANN., Bus. Occ. & Prof. §21-102 (West 2009).

[50] MD. Dep't. of Labor, Licensing & Regulation, *Important Information on the Maryland Individual Tax Preparers Act*, http://dllr.maryland.gov/license/taxprep/.

Under the Maryland Individual Tax Preparers Act, individuals will be registered by examination, which must be no less stringent than the "individuals" section of the special enrollment examination for enrolled agents.[51] Registrants must complete eight hours of continuing education annually and will be required to renew their licenses every two years.[52]

The Board of Individual Tax Return Preparers is authorized to deny registration, to reprimand registered individuals, or to suspend or revoke registration for fraudulently obtaining registration, engaging in criminal activity, or engaging in professional misconduct in violation of rules of conduct to be adopted by the Board.[53] The Board also is authorized to impose penalties up to $5,000 for each violation.[54]

IV. New York

The New York legislature provided the New York Department of Taxation and Finance statutory authority to register tax return preparers.[55] Under New York law, tax return preparers are individuals who prepare a substantial portion of any return for compensation.[56] Tax return preparers include enrolled agents; employees of tax return preparation business; and partners who prepare returns for clients of a partnership engaged in a commercial tax return preparation business.[57] Tax return preparers do not include certified public accountants or public accountants currently licensed in New York State; attorneys currently licensed in New York State; employees who are preparing tax returns under the direct supervision of a certified public accountant, public accountant, or attorney licensed in New York State; employees of a business who prepare that business' return; clerical employees; and volunteer tax preparers.[58] Facilitators of refund anticipation loans or refund anticipation checks must register annually.[59]

Tax return preparers and facilitators must register electronically with the Tax Department and thereafter re-register annually.[60] In addition, at the time of registration or re-registration, commercial tax return preparers must pay a $100 fee.[61] Tax return preparers or facilitators are liable for a $250 penalty for failure to register or re-register, but the penalty will be abated if the registration requirement is met within 90 days.[62] A

---

[51] MD. CODE ANN., Bus. Occ. & Prof. §21-304 (West 2009).
[52] MD. CODE ANN., Bus. Occ. & Prof. §§21-308 and 21-309 (West 2009).
[53] MD. CODE ANN., Bus. Occ. & Prof. §21-311 (West 2009).
[54] Id.
[55] N.Y. Tax §32(b)(1) (McKinney 2009).
[56] N.Y. Tax §32(a)(14) (McKinney 2009).
[57] Id. Commercial tax return preparers are tax return preparers who prepared 10 or more returns in the preceding year and will prepare at least one in the current year, or who prepared 10 or fewer returns in the preceding year and will preparer 10 or more in the current year. N.Y. Tax §32(a)(4) (McKinney 2009).
[58] N.Y. Tax §32(a)(14) (McKinney 2009).
[59] N.Y. Tax §32(b)(1) (McKinney 2009).
[60] N.Y. Tax §32(b)(3)(McKinney 2009).
[61] N.Y. Tax §32(c)(1) (McKinney 2009).
[62] N.Y. Tax §32(g)(1) (McKinney 2009).

$500 penalty applies to failure to register or re-register after the 90-day period and for each additional month thereafter.[63]

Each tax return preparer and facilitator who registers will be issued a certificate and will be assigned an identification number.[64] The issuance of a certificate or the assignment of an identification number cannot be advertised as the Tax Department's endorsement of the tax return preparer's or facilitator's qualifications or services.[65]

C.   Calls for Increased Regulation of Tax Return Preparers

Various organizations that have observed the tax preparation methods and choices available to taxpayers have questioned how taxpayers with limited tax law knowledge themselves can make a knowing assessment of a tax return preparer's competency when anyone, regardless of training, experience, skill or knowledge may prepare federal tax returns for a fee.

I.   National Taxpayer Advocate

The National Taxpayer Advocate is a proponent of tax return preparer regulation, devoting a significant amount of time to raising awareness of this issue in Congress, the IRS, and the public. The National Taxpayer Advocate has raised the issue in her annual reports to Congress since 2002.[66]

The National Taxpayer Advocate advocates strengthening the professionalism of those who prepare tax returns for compensation, not limiting or reducing their numbers. According to the National Taxpayer Advocate, the professionalism of tax return preparers can be increased through a framework that provides for registration, testing, certification, continuing education, and consumer education. Figure 7 outlines four recommendations made by the National Taxpayer Advocate.

---

[63] Id.

[64] N.Y. Tax §32(b)(2)(McKinney 2009).

[65] N.Y. Tax §32(d)(McKinney 2009).

[66] The National Taxpayer Advocate's Annual Reports to Congress are available on the IRS webpage at www.irs.gov/advocate/article/0,,id=97404,00.html.

Figure 7 – National Taxpayer Advocate's Recommendations on Paid Preparers

- Any tax return preparer as defined in IRC § 7701(a)(36) other than an attorney, certified public accountant, or enrolled agent must register with the IRS, and Congress should authorize the IRS to impose a per-return penalty for failure to register, absent reasonable cause.

- All registered preparers must pass an initial examination designed by the Secretary to test the technical knowledge and competency of unenrolled return preparers to prepare federal tax returns. The exam can be administered in two separate parts. The first part would address the technical knowledge required to prepare relatively less complex Form 1040-series returns. The second part would test the technical knowledge required to prepare business returns, including complex sole proprietorship schedules.

- All registered preparers must complete CPE requirements as specified by the Secretary. And all registered preparers must renew their registration every three years, at which point they must show evidence of completion of CPE requirements.

- The Secretary should be authorized and directed to conduct a public awareness campaign to inform the public about the registration requirements and offer guidelines about what taxpayers should look for in choosing a qualified tax return preparer.

The National Taxpayer Advocate proposes to require individuals other than attorneys, certified public accountants, and enrolled agents to pass an IRS examination to prepare federal tax returns. The test would be administered in two parts. Individuals who pass the first part of the examination, addressing technical issues arising on simpler individual tax returns, would be authorized to prepare less complex Form 1040 series returns. Individuals who pass the first and second part of the examination would be authorized to prepare any income tax return. Individuals who pass the examination and prepare returns would be subject to oversight by the IRS. Failure to comply with IRS rules would subject the individual to penalties. Tax return preparers would be required to complete continuing education to renew their registration.

II.   IRS Advisory Organizations

In 2006, the Taxpayer Advocacy Panel recommended licensing of paid tax return preparers.[67] In support of their recommendation, the Taxpayer Advocacy Panel noted that taxpayers are hurt when their returns are not prepared accurately. The Taxpayer Advocacy Panel also argued that the IRS would benefit from the licensing of paid return

---

[67] Taxpayer Advocacy Panel, *2006 Annual Report*, Appendix E (2006).

preparers because the IRS also incurs costs because of fraudulent and inaccurate returns.

The Internal Revenue Service Advisory Council considered the issue of identification of paid tax return preparers in 2008.[68] Noting that the IRS does not have a single database or other information source to identify the paid tax return preparer community, IRSAC recommended that the IRS develop a system to identify all paid tax return preparers through the use of a unique identification number. IRSAC also recommended that the IRS conduct research to effectuate a better process to monitor and regulate the paid tax return preparer community utilizing these unique identification numbers. IRSAC suggested that "these measures should lead to more accurately prepared tax returns and would enable the IRS to provide focused resources for outreach and education efforts."

Most recently, in June 2009, the Electronic Tax Administration Advisory Committee recommended the IRS establish threshold standards and a related oversight model to support integrity in tax preparation software and the e-file industry.[69] ETAAC acknowledged that it is cost and resource prohibitive for the IRS to provide total oversight and regulation of tax preparation software products. Nevertheless, ETAAC suggested the IRS determine the best model for the efficient, effective oversight of tax software services. ETAAC further suggested that IRS select a security standard for IRS authorized e-file providers from among several existing, recognized standards. And, most notably, ETAAC recommended that the IRS work with the tax return preparation industry and States to set high industry standards that will enhance the accuracy of return preparation software.

III. Industry Stakeholders and Consumer Groups

The IRS Oversight Board sponsored a public meeting on the issue of tax return preparer regulation in February 2008. The panelists at the public meeting represented industry stakeholders and consumer advocacy groups.[70] According to the panelists, tax return preparation is a profession, not a part-time job during tax filing season. The panelists explained that, as professionals, most tax return preparers want to protect their profession. Thus, according to the panelists, most tax return preparers favor entry-level requirements, enforcement and penalties for those who do not comply with regulations, although the panelists' views varied on how a regulatory program could be

---

[68] Internal Revenue Service Advisory Council, *General Report* (2008), http://www.irs.gov.taxpros/article/0,,id=188469,00.html.

[69] Electronic Tax Administration Advisory Committee, *Annual Report to Congress* (June 2009), http://www.irs.gov/pub/irs-pdf/p3415.pdf.

[70] Panelists included Robert Tobias, Chair, Internal Revenue Service Oversight Board Operations Committee (Moderator); Kevin R. Keller, Chief Executive Officer, Certified Financial Planner Board of Standards; Michael A. Addington, Federation of Tax Administrators; John Ams, Executive Vice-President, National Society of Accountants; Frank Degen, Past President and Spokesperson, National Association of Enrolled Agents; and Bonnie Speedy, National Director, AARP Foundation Tax-Aide Program.

structured and implemented. Most panelists agreed that there should be an examination for certification, continuing professional education, an ethics requirement, an enforcement component, and user fees.

D.   Legislative Proposals

For several years, bills requiring the registration and regulation of tax return preparers have been introduced and considered in Congress.[71] The sponsors of these bills suggest that passage is long overdue.[72] They argue that the current tax return preparer environment is inadequate because it leaves taxpayers vulnerable to abuses from unqualified or unethical individuals who present themselves as tax professionals.[73] According to the 2007 bill's sponsors, everyone, including the many tax return preparers who provide professional and much needed services to their clients, benefits from the reforms in these bills.[74] They explain that increased tax return preparer regulation will ensure that taxpayers are better able to prepare and file their tax returns in a manner that is fair, reasonable and affordable.[75]

The 2007 legislative proposal would have required the IRS to develop standards for persons to prepare returns commercially.[76] Any individual other than an attorney or certified public accountant would have been required to pass a minimum competency examination to prepare returns for a fee. These individuals also would have been required to complete continuing education to renew their credentials. Further, the IRS could have imposed a penalty on any person who prepared a return for a fee without obtaining the necessary credentials.

STAKEHOLDER AND PUBLIC OPINION

The IRS is committed to a transparent and open dialogue about the issues concerning tax return preparers and tax return preparation. From the Commissioner's June 2009 announcement that he planned to make recommendations to better leverage the tax return preparer community with the twin goals of increasing taxpayer compliance and ensuring uniform and high ethical standards of conduct for tax preparers, the IRS has sought the input of a large and diverse community of internal and external stakeholders.

---

[71] See, *e.g.*, S. 802, *Low Income Taxpayer Protection Act of 2001*, 107th Cong. § 2 (2001); H.R. 1528 (incorporating S. 882), *Tax Administration Good Government Act*, 108th Cong. § 141 (2004); S. 1321 (incorporating S. 832), *Telephone Excise Tax Repeal Act of 2005,* 109th Cong. § 203 (2005); S. 1219, *Taxpayer Protection and Assistance Act of 2007*, 110th Cong. § 4 (2007); H.R. 5716, *Taxpayer Bill of Rights Act of 2008*, 110th Cong. § 4 (2008).
[72] See, *e.g.*, 153 Cong. Rec. S. 5101-5103 (statement of Rep. Bingaman).
[73] Id.
[74] Id.
[75] Id.
[76] S. 1219, Taxpayer Protection and Assistance Act of 2007, 110th Cong. (2007).

The IRS used numerous channels including public forums, solicitation of written comments, and meetings with advisory groups to obtain this input.

A.   Public Forums

The IRS sponsored three public forums featuring panelists representing consumer advocacy groups, tax professional organizations, federal and state government agencies, the software industry, and the retail and unenrolled tax return preparer community. Each forum began with panelists making a short prepared statement.   The forums continued with an open discussion moderated by IRS officials. Complete transcripts for each forum are available on the IRS website.[77]

I.   July 30, 2009, Public Forum

The IRS held the first public forum on July 30, 2009, in Washington D.C. Two panels representing consumer advocacy and tax professional organizations shared their perspectives and positions on the regulation of federal tax return preparers. The organizations represented on the panels included:

Consumer Advocacy Panel:

- National Community Tax Coalition
- Center on Budget and Policy Priorities
- American Association of Retired Persons
- Consumer Federation of America
- The Community Tax Law Project

Tax Professional Panel:

- National Association of Enrolled Agents
- American Institute of Certified Public Accountants
- American Bar Association
- National Society of Accountants
- National Association of Tax Professionals

In addition to the panelists, approximately 200 people registered and attended this open forum.

Consumer Panel Summary:

The representatives from consumer advocacy organizations all recommended that the IRS should increase its oversight of tax return preparers. All five panelists spoke about the benefits of registering tax return preparers. Four of the five panelists also spoke of the additional value of including a testing requirement for unenrolled tax return

---

[77] The agendas for each forum are reprinted in Appendices of this report.

preparers. Three panelists referenced the existing testing requirement for IRS Volunteer Income Tax Assistance (VITA) volunteers. These panelists insisted that the VITA program establishes a process of standardization for what taxpayers can expect from tax return preparers that also should be followed by the paid tax return preparer community.

The consumer advocacy panelists also expressed their concern about refund anticipation loans. A few panelists were particularly vocal. These panelists expressed concern that RALs are marketed mostly to low-income taxpayers and involve annual percentage rates ranging from 50 to nearly 500 percent. The panelists noted that RALs, because of their high annual percentage rates, attract "fringe financial outlets" to tax return preparation including businesses such as payday loan stores, and check cashers. According to these panelists, fringe tax return preparers are a fundamental problem because of the questionable quality of tax return preparation.

Tax Professional Panel Summary:

The tax professional organization representatives were uniform in their support for increased IRS oversight of tax return preparers. Each panelist commented on the appropriateness of requiring registration and use of a unique identification number for all tax return preparers. The panelists agreed on the benefits of some type of competency testing for those individuals not already holding a certification or having a minimum amount of experience. The panelists also suggested that regulated professionals who have demonstrated competence through licensing could be deemed to have demonstrated the minimum competence to prepare returns.

Other areas of agreement included the necessity of enforcement and taxpayer education programs and the benefits of continuing professional education for tax return preparers. The panelists advised that the best way to ensure that those who want to ignore the law comply with any new requirements is to ensure that they suffer financial harm if they flout these requirements.

The tax professional organizations made a variety of comments on the recommended structure for oversight. One panelist, for example, supported the establishment of an administrative entity to oversee tax return preparers, while another panelist insisted that the program build on the existing regulatory framework and consolidate administration and enforcement under the Office of Professional Responsibility.

Finally, the tax professional organizations reminded the IRS to consider burden and avoid unnecessary duplications. They strongly advised against any strategy that would impose duplicative regulatory regimes on attorneys, certified public accountants and enrolled agents.

II.   September 2, 2009, Public Forum

The IRS held its second IRS public forum on September 2, 2009, in Washington D.C. A panel representing federal and state government agencies presented their findings and experiences related to oversight of tax return preparers. The organizations represented included:

Government Panel:

- Government Accountability Office (GAO)
- Treasury Inspector General for Tax Administration (TIGTA)
- Oregon State Board of Tax Practitioners
- California Franchise Tax Board
- California Tax Education Council
- Comptroller of Maryland Revenue Administration Division
- New York Department of Taxation and Finance

In addition to the panelists, approximately 125 persons registered and attended this open forum.

Across the board, the government panelists strongly supported increased IRS oversight of tax return preparers. A few panelists cited examples from GAO and TIGTA investigations as evidence that increased oversight is needed. The panelists from the various States presented background on how their agencies have implemented various levels of regulation involving tax return preparers.

Panelists recommended that the IRS develop a plan to require a single identification number for paid tax return preparers as a first step. One panelist suggested that the IRS expand the use of preparer tax identification numbers to create a unique number for each tax return preparer.

While California and Oregon have had tax return preparer programs in place significantly longer than Maryland and New York, all of the state panelists suggested that their tax return preparer regulations have a positive impact on tax administration. The state panelists also expressed support for stronger federal oversight. They each suggested that their State stands ready to work with the IRS to achieve meaningful oversight of the tax return preparation industry.

III.   September 30, 2009, Public Forum

The IRS held its third and final public forum on September 30, 2009, in Chicago, Illinois. Two panels representing the tax return preparation software industry and independent tax return preparers weighed in with information about their current practices and their opinions about tax return preparation in the U.S. The organizations represented on the panels included:

28

Software Industry Panel:

- Council for Electronic Revenue Communication Advancement
- CCH Small Firm Services
- Drake Software
- Intuit, Inc.

Independent Tax Return Preparer Panel:

- H&R Block executive
- H&R Block franchisee
- Jackson Hewitt franchisee
- Empire Accounting & Tax Service owner
- An independent unenrolled preparer

In addition to the panelists, approximately 140 persons registered and attended the open forum.

Software Industry Panel Summary:

The tax return preparation software industry panelists all agreed on the importance of tax preparation software in today's U.S. tax system and the need for increased oversight of tax return preparers. Yet, the panelists had a range of opinions on the level of IRS or government involvement in this oversight.

Some panelists supported increased IRS involvement in tax return preparation software oversight. But, these panelists recommended against day-to-day involvement by the IRS, suggesting, instead, that the increased oversight be IRS approved standards and certification requirements carried out through a formal self-regulatory organization operating outside the government.

Other panelists encouraged a careful approach to any changes under consideration. These panelists explained that the software market is a competitive market that has and will continue to dictate both the design and cost of these software programs. They noted that if the software is not accurate and compliant, customers will find software that is.

Independent Preparer Panel Summary:

The independent preparer panel included an H&R Block executive who represented her organization and Jackson Hewitt – the nation's two largest tax preparation companies – from a corporate standpoint. Four local tax return preparers representing the unlicensed community of tax return preparers completed the panel.

The panelists recommended registration of all tax return preparers. They also supported some type of qualification standards to demonstrate a minimum level of competency and high ethical standards, noting that their companies and employees already do this. For example, although H&R Block and Jackson Hewitt's 155,000 tax preparers may be primarily unlicensed individuals, the panelists noted that these companies have extensive training and continuing education requirements for their employees. The independent panelists noted that they and many other independent tax return preparers regularly attend educational seminars and classes to ensure they maintain the expertise required to serve their customers. The panelists recognized, however, that based on media and government reports, not all tax return preparers are conducting business in a professional manner. Accordingly, the panelists all appeared to support a federal standard of tax return preparer registration and qualification.

B. Notice 2009-60

On July 24, 2009, the IRS announced that the public was invited to contribute ideas as part of its effort to ensure high performance standards for all tax return preparers.[78] To cast the widest net possible for comment, the IRS chose to solicit written comments. In IRS Notice 2009-60,[79] the IRS specifically requested comments on how the tax return preparer community can assist in increasing taxpayer compliance and how to ensure that tax return preparers meet both uniform and high ethical standards of conduct. The IRS welcomed all ideas but was particularly interested in comments regarding:

• The types of individuals, entities, and professionals who currently work as tax return preparers;
• The level of current regulation of these various categories of tax return preparers and who monitors them;
• Minimum levels of education and training necessary to provide tax return preparation services;
• Whether tax return preparers should be subject to a code of ethics, and, if so, what specific behavior should that code promote or prohibit;
• The responsibility firms or businesses that employ tax return preparers should have for the conduct of the individuals they employ;
• The responsibility tax return preparer professional organizations should have for the education, training, and conduct of their members;
• Special provisions that should be made for individuals who are already tax return preparers, licensed attorneys, certified public accountants, enrolled agents, or software providers if tax return preparation services should be regulated;

---

[78] IRS News Release IR 2009-68 (July 24, 2009).
[79] 2009-32 IRB 181 (Aug. 10, 2009).

• Additional legislative, regulatory, or administrative rules the IRS should consider recommending as part of its proposals with respect to the tax return preparer community.

The IRS received more than 500 comments in response to this solicitation.[80] The backgrounds of the respondents are diverse, covering all categories of affected individuals and entities. The IRS heard from hundreds of individual tax return preparers and taxpayers in addition to receiving comments from dozens of tax professional organizations, consumer advocacy groups, commercial tax return preparation firms, and commercial tax return preparation software providers. The overwhelming majority of respondents favor some level of increased regulation. Highlights from an IRS analysis of the responses include:

- 98 percent of the individuals who offered comments on oversight and enforcement for paid tax return preparers favor increased efforts;
- 88 percent of the individuals who expressed an opinion on registering paid tax return preparers favor registration;
- 90 percent of the individuals who commented on education and testing favor minimum education or testing requirements for paid tax return preparers;
- 98 percent of the individuals who commented on quality and ethics favor establishment of quality and ethics standards for paid tax return preparers;
- 99 percent of the individuals who provided comments on outreach and communication for paid tax return preparers favor increased efforts.

Notwithstanding this tremendous support for increased IRS oversight of tax return preparers, a few commenters considered increased oversight a waste of time and money. A few commenters rejected the suggestion that tax return preparers be tested, noting that the IRS and tax return preparer community are doing a good job of policing tax return preparers currently via audits and reviews. These commenters suggested that the "bad apples" eventually come to light. Some commenters expressed concern that the intent of any increased oversight not be to "squeeze out" the unlicensed tax return preparer who has been conducting themselves competently and professionally over the years. These commenters wanted to ensure that individuals who prepare simple Form 1040 would not be subject to examination and regulation inconsistent with the returns that they prepare.

The commenters also offered different views on the form of any increased oversight. Many commenters, for example, supported the view of the National Taxpayer Advocate and consumer advocacy groups who advocate for a regulatory framework that includes registration, testing, continuing education, and consumer education. Other commenters believed that testing should not be part of the framework because it is not the solution to incompetent return preparation. To these commenters, the issue is compliance and that

---

[80] Comments to Notice 2009-60 are posted on the IRS webpage at www.irs.gov/taxpros/article/0,,id=212569,00.html.

compliance can be adequately addressed through registration and ethical standards, not testing.

For those who supported testing, another issue of concern was "grandfathering." Proponents of "grandfathering" suggested that many unlicensed tax return preparers have been preparing accurate returns for several years with little to no problems with the IRS. These tax return preparers, they argued, have been obtaining continuing professional education and kept current with the tax literature and should be given a pass on any testing requirements. Several enrolled agents, attorneys and certified public accountants argued against "grandfathering," noting that a minimum level of competency needs to be assured through examination. Many attorneys, certified public accountants and enrolled agents expressed concern, however, about duplicative regulation for those tax return preparers who hold professional licenses or are authorized to practice before the IRS and are subject to IRS and State regulation currently. But, other commenters raised the specter of fairness if certain tax return preparers were exempted from any new requirements because of their professional licenses.

Commenters also offered ideas about enforcement. Some commenters suggested new penalties for those individuals who prepare returns without a license. Others suggested raising the current penalties for tax return preparers who prepare inaccurate returns. A few commenters suggested 'A Paid Tax Preparer Registry' on the IRS webpage where members of the public could find a list of registered tax return preparers, research a tax return preparer for possible complaints or judgments against them, and report tax return preparers who violated the law or provided unacceptable service. Commenters also spoke of a code of ethics for tax return preparers with many suggesting that tax return preparers should be subject to Circular 230 or a code of ethics similar to the one in Circular 230.

A few commenters expressed concern about the cost of increased regulation and who would bear the responsibility for incurring the additional costs.

FINDINGS AND RECOMMENDATIONS

Over the past 6 months, the IRS, tax return preparers, the associated industry, other federal and state government officials, consumer advocacy groups and the American public engaged in a transparent and open dialogue about tax return preparation in this country. Three public forums were held and more than 500 individuals and groups offered written comments. The results of this discussion are, in many ways, remarkable. There is general agreement that tax return preparers and the associated industry play a pivotal role in our system of tax administration and they must be a part of any strategy to strengthen the integrity of the tax system. And, more directly, the American public overwhelmingly supports efforts to increase the oversight of paid tax return preparers.

The IRS believes that increased oversight of paid tax return preparers does not require additional legislation. As discussed more fully below, the IRS' intention is to require paid tax return preparers to register with the IRS through the issuance of regulations under section 6109 of the Internal Revenue Code. Further, the IRS considers the preparation of a tax return for compensation as a form of representation before the agency. Thus, the IRS intends to amend the regulations under 31 U.S.C. 330 to clarify that any person preparing a tax return for compensation is practicing before the agency and, therefore, must demonstrate good character, good reputation, and the necessary qualifications and competency to advise and assist other persons in the preparation of their federal tax returns. The IRS, therefore, is recommending the following:

A. Mandatory Registration for Tax Return Preparers

Increased oversight begins with mandatory registration. Almost 90 percent of those persons expressing an opinion on registration favored registering all paid tax return preparers. Registration of all tax return preparers will enable the IRS to collect more accurate data on return preparers. Additionally, registration will help the IRS provide better service to the tax return preparer community and taxpayers generally. For example, by tracking the number of persons who prepare returns, the qualifications of those who are preparing returns and the number of returns each person prepares, the IRS will be able to send targeted updates to those tax return preparers who have clients that are most likely to be impacted by significant or late changes in the tax laws or IRS procedures. Additionally, registration will make it easier for the IRS to locate and review the returns prepared by a tax return preparer when instances of misconduct are detected.

All tax return preparers are required to furnish an identifying number on any return that they are required to sign as a paid tax return preparer. Currently, the signing tax return preparer may provide either a social security number or a preparer tax identification number that the IRS will issue to the tax return preparer on application. The use of more than one number by any signing tax return preparer, however, makes it more difficult for the IRS to collect accurate tax return preparer data and to identify an individual tax return preparer. The IRS, therefore, intends to require all individuals who prepare returns for compensation and are required to sign those returns to register and obtain a preparer tax identification number. The IRS may charge a reasonable, nonrefundable fee to register as a tax return preparer. All tax return preparers will be required to provide their preparer tax identification number on any tax return that they prepare and sign for compensation.

Registration will be phased in to reduce burden on both the IRS and tax return preparers. Tax return preparers also will be required to renew their registration every three years. All tax return preparers will be required to pay a user fee to register and when they renew their registration. Tax return preparers also will be subject to a tax compliance check at the time of each renewal.[81] Although the IRS initially will require only signing tax return preparers to register, it will consider extending the registration requirement to all tax return preparers, and in particular to non-signing tax return preparers who are not attorneys, CPAs, enrolled agents, or otherwise licensed as tax professionals.

The renewal requirement will assist the IRS in collecting accurate identifying information on tax return preparers. For example, to better understand who is preparing returns, the IRS proposes to collect information regarding a tax return preparer's professional qualifications and current employment. The IRS also intends to request updated contact information when the tax return preparer renews his or her registration.

B. Competency Examination Requirement

Most commenters favored competency examinations for tax return preparers. The commenters do not agree, however, on who should be tested. Many attorneys, certified public accountants and enrolled agents support testing for those who are not required to pass examinations to obtain their professional credentials. They argue that testing of those who had to pass examinations to obtain their professional credentials would be costly and redundant. Other commenters noted, however, that many of these professionals passed examinations that have no bearing on the professional's ability to prepare a tax return, although their ethical standards require that they not offer or provide services that they are not qualified to provide. Some commenters disagreed with testing or offered only lukewarm support. Other commenters appeared resigned to the idea that testing was going to be implemented and merely held out hope that those with significant return preparation experience and no known issues would be "grandfathered" from any testing requirement.

In addition to the commenters' support for testing, government studies reveal that a number of return preparers are not always preparing accurate returns.   Similarly, a recent undercover effort by the State of New York Department of Taxation and Finance resulted in 20 arrests and 13 convictions for unethical and criminal behavior in the first 20 months. Although the samples for these studies are too limited to make broad pronouncements about tax return preparers generally, they can not be overlooked when discussing the need for competency testing.

The IRS is proposing to establish competency testing for tax return preparers who are not attorneys, certified public accountants, or enrolled agents. The IRS is not proposing a competency testing program for attorneys, certified public accountants, or enrolled

---

[81] For renewal of registration purposes, a tax compliance check is a limited review of the tax return preparer's filing and payment compliance history (i.e., the IRS will ensure that the tax return preparer has filed his or her federal personal and business tax returns and that the tax due on those returns has been paid or the tax return preparer has reached an acceptable agreement with the IRS to satisfy any outstanding liabilities). Those tax return preparers who are not in compliance will be referred to the IRS Office of Professional Responsibility for possible disciplinary action.

agents currently, but the IRS will consider expanding testing to those individuals if data is collected in the future that identifies a need for this testing.

Initially, two examinations will be offered for tax return preparers who are not attorneys, certified public accountants, or enrolled agents. The first test will cover wage and nonbusiness income Form 1040 series returns. The second test will cover wage and small business income Form 1040 series returns. The proposed content for two examinations is shown in Appendix I. The IRS will not "grandfather" any tax return preparer from the testing requirement based on return preparation experience.

During the roll-out of the initial testing that will require return preparers to take one of two examinations relating to Form 1040 issues, the IRS will closely monitor the implementation of the testing requirements. The IRS plans to add a third competency examination for return preparers after the initial implementation phase is completed. The third competency examination will address business tax issues.

Additionally, although attorneys, certified public accountants, and enrolled agents are asked to demonstrate their good character before they obtain their professional license or are enrolled to practice, many tax return preparers are not required to make any showing of character before they prepare returns. Consumer advocacy groups and many commenters expressed concern about the lack of regulation in this regard. Thus, the IRS intends to perform suitability checks[82] when these individuals make their initial application to take the competency examination.

Although the IRS believes that testing of paid tax return preparers who are not attorneys, certified public accountants, or enrolled agents is essential, the testing must be administered in a way that avoids significant interruption of service to taxpayers. The IRS, therefore, proposes that these tax return preparers be given three years from the initial implementation date of testing to pass the required examination(s).[83] Also, tax return preparers testing during this initial implementation period may attempt to pass the examination as often as the examination is offered provided the applicable fee is paid for each attempt.

C. Continuing Professional Education

Continuing professional education requirements serve to encourage professionals to remain current and to expand their knowledge within their field of expertise. These requirements are important to tax administration given the complexity of the tax laws and the frequent changes made to the Internal Revenue Code and the rules and regulations implemented to assist in the administration of the Code.

---

[82] Suitability checks may include criminal background checks and tax compliance checks. For purposes of a suitability check, a tax compliance check is a limited review of the tax return preparer's filing and payment compliance history.

[83] Individuals required to pass the examination(s) will be permitted to register as tax return preparers and receive a preparer tax identification number during this initial implementation even if they have not passed the examination(s).

Commenters generally supported continuing professional education requirements for return preparers. Several commenters noted that most attorneys, certified public accountants, enrolled agents, and state registered tax return preparers currently must complete continuing education to retain their professional credentials (Figure 8). In addition, certain tax return preparers who are not licensed and do not hold professional credentials are members of organizations that have minimum continuing education requirements. For example, one organization of accountants requires that its members complete 72 hours of continuing professional education over three years, with a minimum of 16 hours per year. These commenters generally supported continuing education requirements for those tax return preparers who were not required to complete continuing education already.

Figure 8 – Existing Continuing Education Requirements

Certification	Continuing education requirement
Attorney	Varies by state – 10 to 15 hours per year is average
Certified Public Accountant	Varies by state – ranges from 120 hours over 3 years to 20 per year
Enrolled Agent	72 hours over 3 years; 16 hours minimum per year including 2 hours ethics/professional conduct
California registered preparer	20 hours per year
Oregon registered preparer	30 hours per year

The IRS believes that all tax return preparers have an obligation to stay current on the tax laws. The IRS, therefore, proposes that return preparers complete 15 hours of continuing professional education annually. Of the 15 hours of continuing professional education, the IRS proposes that three hours cover federal tax law updates (including recent legislation and updates to IRS procedures), two hours cover ethics, and 10 hours cover general federal tax law topics. Because most attorneys, certified public accountants, enrolled agents, enrolled actuaries and enrolled retirement plan agents must complete continuing education to retain their professional credentials, these individuals will be exempted from the tax return preparers' continuing professional education requirements. The IRS will consider requiring the completion of tax return preparer continuing professional education from these individuals if data is collected in the future that identifies a need for this educational requirement. Additionally, the IRS will reach out to their licensing authorities to encourage them to support annual continuing professional education that includes federal tax law topics and updates and ethics for those individuals who are licensed by them and who prepare federal tax returns.

D.   Ethical Standards

Almost all commenters who had an opinion on ethical standards favored the establishment of ethics standards for return preparers. Most of these commenters suggested that tax return preparers be required to follow the standard of conduct found in Treasury Department Circular 230. Other commenters expressed concern about bringing all tax return preparers under the umbrella of Circular 230 if that means those who are not attorneys, certified public accountants, enrolled agents, enrolled actuaries or enrolled retirement plan agents would be authorized to practice before the IRS without meeting the current requirements for enrolled agents, enrolled actuaries or enrolled retirement plan agents.

The IRS agrees with the overwhelming majority of commenters that tax return preparers must be covered by a standard of ethics. The IRS is proposing to require all signing and nonsigning tax return preparers to comply with the standard of conduct in Part 10 of Title 31 of the Code of Federal Regulations and reprinted in Treasury Department Circular 230. The authority of attorneys, certified public accountants, enrolled agents, enrolled actuaries and enrolled retirement plan agents to practice before the IRS will not change from the authority they have under current Treasury Department Circular 230. The remaining tax return preparers will be authorized to prepare returns and to represent a client before the IRS during an examination of any return that the tax return preparer prepared for the client as they are currently permitted under the limited practice provisions in section 10.7(viii) of Treasury Department Circular 230. The conduct of the tax return preparer in connection with the preparation of the return and any representation of the client during an examination will be subject to standard of conduct in Treasury Department Circular 230. Further, inquiries into possible misconduct and disciplinary proceedings relating to tax return preparer misconduct will be conducted under Treasury Department Circular 230.

E.   Tax Return Preparer Enforcement

Most commenters observed that increased IRS oversight of tax return preparers will require a strong enforcement program. Without a strong enforcement program, some commenters suggested that taxpayers could be misled. According to these commenters, taxpayers will assume that the new standards are being enforced and they will rely on this assumption when they choose a tax return preparer. If individuals believe that the IRS will not detect noncompliance or sanction those who are not compliant, tax return preparers and taxpayers will lose confidence in the standards and may have an incentive not to comply. Increased IRS oversight of tax return preparers, therefore, must include a strong enforcement mechanism that has sufficient resources to assure its long-term viability and credibility.

The IRS will develop a comprehensive, service-wide enforcement strategy that utilizes data gathered through registration and other means to address individuals who fail to comply with the new IRS paid preparer regulations. This strategy will include the issuance of new policy guidance that applies significant examination and collection resources to tax return preparer compliance. Additionally, the IRS intends to strengthen the relationships and coordination among its business units relating to tax return preparer compliance issues.

The strategy will also include the IRS looking at ways to enhance the effectiveness of its traditional enforcement tools against tax return preparers (*e.g.*, tax return preparer and promoter penalties, program action cases, and injunctions). For example, the IRS intends to elevate the priority of tax return preparer penalties in Collection.

Further, the IRS proposes to recommend that the period of limitations under section 6696(d) for assessing a penalty under sections 6694(a), 6695 and 6695A be extended. The IRS is not recommending any new penalties or an increase in any penalty amounts currently, but will continue to study whether a recommendation might be appropriate in the future.

The IRS intends to incorporate new enforcement tools into its enforcement strategy. For example, the IRS will consider the use of targeted notices that call on tax return preparers to correct situations of noncompliance. If the tax return preparer self corrects the noncompliance, the IRS may not pursue penalties. The IRS also intends to more widely utilize preparer visits to identify tax return preparer noncompliance. Currently, the IRS only performs earned income tax credit preparer visits and electronic return originator visits. Further, the IRS will increase the staffing of the Office of Professional Responsibility to allow for more investigations of practitioner, including tax return preparer, misconduct.

The IRS believes that increased tax return preparer compliance will increase taxpayer compliance generally. However, the IRS recognizes that increased tax return preparer compliance will not address all taxpayer compliance issues. The IRS, therefore, continues to explore ways to enhance overall taxpayer compliance. The IRS is particularly focused on improving enforcement in areas where acknowledged issues exist (*e.g.*, earned income tax credit, international taxation).

The IRS is cognizant that the robust enforcement of tax return preparer compliance will require resources. The IRS, therefore, plans to study the impact an enhanced tax return preparer enforcement strategy has on other enforcement initiatives and taxpayer compliance generally. Dependent on the outcomes realized, the IRS will consider further changes to its enforcement strategy to maximize the use of its enforcement resources.

F.   Tax Return Preparation Software

The tax software industry has fundamentally changed the means of compliance with our civic tax obligations. There is general agreement that tax administration has benefited from the proliferation of consumer and commercial tax preparation software. There is,

38

however, no consensus on whether tax administration would benefit from increased or enhanced regulation of the tax preparation software industry.

While there have been few studies completed on the quality and accuracy of tax preparation software, some in the industry suggest that the market adequately regulates the industry. According to these stakeholders, if your software is not accurate and compliant, your customers will find software that is. Others, however, acknowledge that there is room for improvement and enhancement in the furtherance of the public interest.

With no consensus on whether enhanced regulation of the tax preparation software industry is necessary and little data available, additional research and planning are recommended. The IRS plans to continue to assess the risks of a high level dependence on consumer and commercial tax preparation software. In furtherance of this goal, the IRS will form a task force that will seek the input of industry representatives, state governments, and other impacted stakeholders. The task force will identify possible risks to tax administration, particularly in the area of tax return accuracy, the security and privacy of taxpayer information and the reliability of electronic filing. The task force will also explore the possibility of establishing industry standards. Research on accuracy issues will be conducted and sources to validate accuracy problems, if any, will be identified and analyzed.

G. Refund Settlement Products

Consumer and taxpayer advocates have long been vocal in their opposition to the use of refund settlement products. These groups charge that changes are needed to protect taxpayers from fraudulent and misleading marketing schemes that conceal the true, high cost of services and loan products.

Some consumer advocates argue that refund settlement products entice fringe tax return preparers, including payday loan stores, and check cashers. Others suggest that the presence of refund settlement products and their pricing structure encourages tax return preparers to take overly aggressive positions on returns to inflate the size of the expected refund and, therefore, the profits to be made from the refund settlement product. Some consumer advocates also criticize the refund settlement industry for misleading sales practices and what they describe as high, unnecessary fees. A recent TIGTA study found that, although taxpayers purchase refund settlement products to obtain quicker access to their refunds, the timing gap between the receipt of the refund settlement product proceeds and the refund may not be great for most.[84] For example; 16 percent of respondents with RALs waited six or more days, and 28 percent of respondents with RALs had to wait at least three days for access to their funds. (See Figure 9 for additional detail.)

---

[84] Treasury Inspector General for Tax Administration, *Many Taxpayers Who Obtain Refund Anticipation Loans Could Benefit From Free Tax Preparation Services*, TIGTA 2008-40-170.

Figure 9: Number of Days Respondents Waited to Receive Their RALs or Refund Anticipation Checks Compared to the Time it Took the IRS to Issue the Refunds

# of Days for Respondents to Receive RALs or RACs	Number of Respondents	Received RALs	Received RACs	# of Days for the IRS to Process Tax Returns/Refunds
Same Day	28 (11%)	6		5 to 7 days
		21		8 to 14 days
1 to 2 Days	103 (41%)	24	1	5 to 7 days
		77	1	8 to 14 days
3 to 5 Days	32 (13%)	6	5	5 to 7 days
		16	5	8 to 14 days
6 to 10 Days	42 (17%)	5	10	5 to 7 days
		11	16	8 to 14 days
11 Days or Longer	45 (18%)	2	8	5 to 7 days
		11	22	8 to 14 days
Totals	**250 (100%)**	**179**	**68**	
Totals	**250**	**247***		

* As of April 17, 2008, three taxpayers had not received their refunds because the tax returns were going through IRS screening.

Source: Treasury Inspector General for Tax Administration, *Many Taxpayers Who Obtain Refund Anticipation Loans Could Benefit From Free Tax Preparation Services,* TIGTA 2008-40-170

In response to concerns about the refund settlement industry, consumer advocates and others have called for a ban or severe restriction of refund settlement products, such as through a statutory prohibition against making loans secured by tax refunds or by the proceeds of specific tax credits, such as the earned income credit. Short of a total ban on refund settlement products, some have proposed eliminating the debt indicator[85], limiting access to the debt indicator, or changing the timing or programming of the debt indicator to limit refund loans.

In order to address widespread concerns about the refund settlement product industry, the IRS will convene a working group to review the refund settlement product industry. Part of this review will include analyzing opportunities available for the improvement of refund delivery options, including those for unbanked taxpayers. The IRS will seek input from industry representatives and consumer advocates during this process. Additionally, the IRS will assess the effectiveness of the debt indicator program and will consider changes to the program, including its possible elimination. The IRS also will explore additional opportunities to improve the efficiency of refund delivery.

---

[85] The IRS ceased providing the debt indicator in the mid-1990s but reinstated in it 1999.

H.   Public Awareness and Service Enhancements

Public awareness and support is a key to the success of increased IRS oversight of tax return preparers. Taxpayers will "vote with their feet" if they can easily discern which tax return preparers are qualified to prepare returns.[86] But, taxpayers are not different than other consumers; they cannot be expected to make the best decisions if they do not have good information. The IRS, therefore, intends to conduct an extensive public awareness campaign to educate taxpayers about the new standards and requirements for tax return preparers.

The IRS will utilize a full range of social media, public service announcements and paid advertising, if authorized, to provide taxpayers with information on what standards the IRS requires of tax return preparers and how they can determine whether their tax return preparer has met these standards. The IRS also intends to leverage its relationships with key industry stakeholders and consumer advocacy groups to have them put the message out that taxpayers should only use a tax return preparer who has met the required standards. The IRS will develop a strategy to ensure that taxpayers and tax return preparers know that the IRS values the role of the tax return preparer community in tax administration and is committed to ongoing collaboration and communication and education enhancements. Finally, the IRS plans to introduce a searchable database of tax return preparers who have met the required standards on its website after the initial registration and examination period have been completed.

---

[86] IRS Oversight Board Taxpayer Attitude Survey, Question 13 (2008).

IRS Launches Tax Return Preparer Review; Recommendations to Improve Compliance Expected by Year End

IR-2009-57, June 4, 2009

WASHINGTON — IRS Commissioner Doug Shulman announced today that by the end of 2009, he will propose a comprehensive set of recommendations to help the Internal Revenue Service better leverage the tax return preparer community with the twin goals of increasing taxpayer compliance and ensuring uniform and high ethical standards of conduct for tax preparers.

Some of the potential recommendations could focus on a new model for the regulation of tax return preparers; service and outreach for return preparers; education and training of return preparers; and enforcement related to return preparer misconduct. The Commissioner will submit recommendations to the Treasury Secretary and the President by the end of the year.

"Tax return preparers help Americans with one of their biggest financial transactions each year. We must ensure that all preparers are ethical, provide good service and are qualified," Shulman said. "At the end the day, tax preparers and the associated industry must be part of our overall game plan to strengthen the integrity of the tax system."

The first part of this groundbreaking effort will involve fact finding and receiving input from a large and diverse constituent community that includes those that are licensed by state and federal authorities – such as enrolled agents, lawyers and accountants – as well as unlicensed tax preparers and software vendors. The effort will also seek input and dialog with consumer groups and taxpayers.

"We plan to have a transparent and open dialogue about the issues," Shulman said. "At this early and critical stage of the process, we need to hear from the broadest possible range of stakeholders."

Later this year, the IRS plans to hold a number of open meetings in Washington and around the country with constituent groups.

More information, including schedules and agendas for public meetings, will be posted on the "Tax Professionals" page on the IRS web site at www.irs.gov, and will be communicated to stakeholder groups.

APPENDIX B

Tax Preparer Review; Public Forums to Gather Input this Summer

IR-2009-66, July 14, 2009

WASHINGTON — The Internal Revenue Service today announced a series of public forums at which individuals and representatives of diverse constituent groups will be able to provide input on the development of tax preparer performance standards.

The public forums, a crucial part of an effort launched in June by IRS Commissioner Doug Shulman to help ensure tax preparers are qualified, ethical and provide a high level of service, will kick off on July 30 in Washington, D.C.

"These public meetings will be an important part of the dialogue as we move toward a set of comprehensive recommendations by the end of this year," Shulman said. "We want an open discussion on how to strengthen the overall integrity of our tax system."

Two panels are scheduled for a forum on July 30. The first panel will give consumer groups an opportunity to provide recommendations. These groups include the AARP, Consumer Federation of America, Center on Budget and Policy Priorities, National Community Tax Coalition and Low Income Tax Clinics.

The second panel will be made up of tax professional groups, including the American Institute of Certified Public Accountants, the National Association of Enrolled Agents, the National Association of Tax Professionals and the National Society of Accountants.

The two panels will take place at the Ronald Reagan Building amphitheater in Washington starting at 9 a.m. on July 30. People interested in attending should confirm attendance by sending an e-mail message to: CL.NPL.Communications@irs.gov.

The IRS also plans to convene meetings with other constituent groups later this summer and fall. Input will be sought from:

- Federal and state organizations

- IRS advisory groups, including the Internal Revenue Service Advisory Committee (IRSAC), the Information Reporting Program Advisory Committee (IRPAC), the Electronic Tax Administration Advisory Committee (ETAAC), the Taxpayer Advocacy Panel (TAP) and the Advisory Committee on Tax Exempt and Government Entities (ACT)

- Unaffiliated and individual tax preparers and groups

- Private firms that support tax preparers

The dates and locations of these meetings will be announced as they become available. Small groups of tax preparers will also have the opportunity this summer to meet with IRS representatives to present their ideas at the IRS Nationwide Tax Forums.

The Nationwide Tax Forums this year include: Orlando, Aug. 4-6; New York, Aug. 25-27; Dallas, Sept. 8-10; and Atlanta, Sept. 22-24.

APPENDIX C

IRS Seeks Public Comment for Proposals to Boost
Tax Preparer Performance Standards

IR-2009-68, July 24, 2009

WASHINGTON — The Internal Revenue Service is inviting the public to contribute ideas as part of an effort to ensure high performance standards for all tax preparers.

Last month, IRS Commissioner Doug Shulman announced plans to develop by year-end a comprehensive set of proposals to ensure consistent standards for tax preparer qualifications, ethics and service. Subsequently, the IRS announced a series of public forums, beginning in Washington, D.C., on July 30, to gather input from various stakeholder groups and organizations.

Two panel discussions involving representatives of consumer groups and tax professional organizations will take place at the Ronald Reagan Building amphitheater in Washington starting at 9 a.m. on July 30. Anyone interested in attending should confirm attendance by sending an e-mail message to:
CL.NPL.Communications@irs.gov.

Notice 2009-60 issued today is an additional call for public comments and helps guarantee that all interested individuals and entities have the opportunity to contribute ideas.

"We are casting a wide net and seeking comment from not only tax preparers and the industry but also from the general public," Shulman said. "We encourage a wide range of people, including taxpayers themselves, to give us their ideas and suggestions."

More than 80 percent of taxpayers use either a paid-preparer or third-party software to prepare their annual tax returns. Professionals who represent clients before the IRS, including attorneys, accountants and enrolled agents are already subject to IRS oversight. But under current law, a much larger group of return preparers are not.

Written comments must be received by Aug. 31, 2009. They should be submitted to CCPA:LPD:PR (Notice 2009-60), Room 5203, Internal Revenue Service, P.O. Box 7604, Ben Franklin Station, Washington, D.C. 20044. Comments may also be e-mailed to: Notice.Comments@irscounsel.treas.gov

Please include "Notice 2009-60" in the subject line of any e-mail messages. More details can be found in IRS Notice 2009-60.

APPENDIX D

Part III - Administrative, Procedural, and Miscellaneous

Standards of Conduct for the Tax Return Preparer Community and Increased Taxpayer Compliance

Notice 2009-60

PURPOSE

This notice invites public comments regarding the Internal Revenue Service's review of issues concerning tax return preparers. In June 2009, the Service announced plans to propose a comprehensive set of recommendations by the end of 2009 regarding how the tax return preparer community can help increase taxpayer compliance and how to ensure that tax return preparers meet both uniform and high ethical standards of conduct. See IR-2009-57 (June 4, 2009). The Service is seeking the input of tax preparers, the associated industry, consumer groups, and taxpayers before any recommendations are made.

To assist in developing its proposals and to ensure that input is received from a broad range of stakeholders, the Service has scheduled a number of meetings in Washington, D.C., and around the country with constituent groups. See IR-2009-66 (July 14, 2009). In this Notice, the Service is requesting written comments from all affected persons and entities. The information collected will assist the Service in drafting recommendations.

REQUESTS FOR PUBLIC COMMENT

The Service requests comments on 1) how the tax return preparer community can assist in increasing taxpayer compliance and 2) how to ensure that tax return preparers meet both uniform and high ethical standards of conduct. The Service is particularly interested in any comments regarding:

• What types of individuals, entities, and professionals currently work as tax return preparers? How are their tax return preparation services currently monitored or regulated by professional organizations or the government? How could this monitoring and regulation be improved?

• How do difference in regulation and oversight affect how the various groups of tax return preparers interact with the Service and taxpayers?

• Is there a minimum level of education and training necessary to provide tax return preparation services? If so, who should be responsible for ensuring that a tax return preparer meets this minimum level and how should that be done?

• What, if any, service and outreach should be provided to tax return preparers and taxpayers? Who should provide (and bear the costs for) these needed services?

• Should tax return preparers be subject to a code of ethics, and, if so, what specific behavior should that code promote or prohibit? How would that code of ethics interact with existing ethical standards that may already be applicable?

• What, if any, responsibility should the firms or businesses that employ tax return preparers have for the conduct of the individuals they employ?

- What, if any, responsibility should tax return preparer professional organizations have for the education, training, and conduct of their members?

- If tax return preparation services should be regulated, what, if any, special regulatory provisions should be made for individuals who are already tax return preparers, licensed attorneys, certified public accountants, enrolled agents, or software providers?

- What, if any, additional legislative, regulatory, or administrative rules should the Service consider recommending as part of its proposals with respect to the tax return preparer community?

Written comments should be sent to: CCPA:LPD:PR (Notice 2009-60), Room 5203, Internal Revenue Service, P.O. Box 7604, Ben Franklin Station, Washington, D.C. 20044. Alternatively, comments may be hand delivered between the hours of 8:00 a.m. and 4:00 p.m. Monday to Friday to CC:PA:LPD:PR (Notice 2009-60), Courier's Desk, Internal Revenue Service, 1111 Constitution Avenue, NW, Washington, D.C. Comments may also be transmitted electronically via the following e-mail address: Notice.Comments@irscounsel.treas.gov. Please include "Notice 2009-60" in the subject line of any electronic communications.

All comments will be available for public inspection and copying. Because the Service intends to make recommendations by December 31, 2009, comments, if any, must be received by August 31, 2009.

DRAFTING INFORMATION

The principal author of this notice is Richard S. Goldstein of the Office of Associate Chief Counsel (Procedure & Administration). For further information regarding this notice contact Richard S. Goldstein at (202) 622-3400 (not a toll free call).

APPENDIX E

IRS Seeks Comments from Government Agencies at Upcoming Public Forum on Proposals to Advance Tax Preparer Performance Standards

IR-2009-74, Aug. 17, 2009

WASHINGTON — The Internal Revenue Service today announced the second in a series of public forums will be held on Wednesday, Sept. 2, in Washington, D.C., and feature a panel of federal and state officials, moderated by IRS Commissioner Doug Shulman.

The panel will include representatives from the Treasury Inspector General for Tax Administration (TIGTA) and the U.S. Governmental Accountability Office (GAO). Representatives from the states of California, Maryland, Oregon and New York will also participate on the panel.

Shulman announced a far-reaching review of paid preparers on June 4 to produce a comprehensive set of recommendations by the end of this year to boost taxpayer compliance and strengthen industry standards.

"This is the next important step in our open dialogue with interested parties in this effort," Shulman said. "I'm very pleased with the quality of the feedback we've received so far. I'm confident these forums will ensure that all ideas are on the table when it's time to form our recommendations."

The forum will convene at 9 a.m. ET in the IRS Headquarters at 1111 Constitution Ave. NW, Washington, DC 20224. Anyone interested in attending should confirm attendance by sending an e-mail message to CL.NPL.Communications@irs.gov.

The first public forum was held on July 30 in Washington, D.C., and featured a panel of consumer groups and another panel of tax professional organizations. A third forum will be held in Chicago on Sept. 30 featuring independent return preparers and software industry representatives.

The IRS issued Notice 2009-60 on July 24 as an added call for public comments to ensure that all interested individuals and entities have the opportunity to contribute ideas.

Written comments must be received by Aug. 31, 2009. They should be submitted to CCPA:LPD:PR (Notice 2009-60), Room 5203, Internal Revenue Service, P.O. Box 7604, Ben Franklin Station, Washington, D.C. 20044.

Comments may also be e-mailed to Notice.Comments@irscounsel.treas.gov. Please include "Notice 2009-60" in the subject line of any e-mail messages. More details can be found in the notice.

Related information

- IR-2009-57
- IR-2009-66
- IR-2009-68
- Notice 2009-60
- Comments from July 30 Forum

Return Preparer Review Public Forum
July 30, 2009
9:00 – 12:00
<u>Agenda</u>

Welcome   *Doug Shulman, Commissioner*

Consumer Panel   *Mark Ernst, Deputy Commissioner, Operations Support*

                                            (Moderator)

> *Introduction of Panel Members*

   o National Community Tax Coalition-Robin McKinney, Director of the Maryland
     CASH Campaign

   o Center on Budget and Policy Priorities – John Wancheck, EITC Campaign
     Coordinator

   o American Association of Retired Persons – Bonnie Speedy, National Director,
     AARP Tax-Aide

   o Consumer Federation of America – Jean Ann Fox, Director of Financial
     Services

   o Low Income Tax Clinic – Paul Harrison, Clinic Coordinator, Community
     Tax Law Project

> *5 Minute Statements*

> *Discussion*

Wrap Up   *Mark Ernst, Deputy Commissioner, Operations Support*
                    Karen L. Hawkins, Director, Office of Professional Responsibility
                    Doug Shulman, Commissioner

15 Minute Break

Preparer Panel   *Karen L. Hawkins, Director, Office of Professional Responsibility*

(Moderator)

➤ *Introduction of Panel Members*

- o   National Association Enrolled Agents – Frank Degen, Chair, Government Relations Committee
- o   The American Institute of Certified Public Accountants – Mike Dolan, Chair, IRS Practice and Procedure Committee of the AICPA
- o   American Bar Association – Armando Gomez, Vice Chair, Government Relations
- o   National Society of Accountants – Jim Nolen, President
- o   National Association of Tax Professionals – Larry Gray, Government Affairs Liaison

➤ *5 Minute Statements*

➤ *Discussion*

Wrap Up   *Karen L. Hawkins, Director, Office of Professional Responsibility*
                Mark Ernst, Deputy Commissioner, Operations Support
                Doug Shulman, Commissioner

Closing   *Doug Shulman, Commissioner*

Return Preparer Review Public Forum
September 2, 2009
9:00 – 11:00
<u>Agenda</u>

Welcome

Doug Shulman, Commissioner

Introduction of Panel Members

*Mark Ernst, Deputy Commissioner, Operations Support
(Moderator)*

*Karen L. Hawkins, Director, Office of Professional Responsibility
(Moderator)*

o   U.S. Government Accountability Office (GAO) - Michael Brostek, Director, Strategic

Issues

o   Treasury Inspector General for Tax Administration (TIGTA) – Mike McKenney,

Assistant Inspector General for Audit

o   California Tax Education Council (CTEC) – Celeste Heritage, CTEC Administrator

o   California Franchise Tax Board – Ruth Moore, Manager, Fraud & Discovery Section,

Filing Compliance Bureau

o   Maryland – Wallace A. Eddleman, Assistant Director-Legal, Comptroller of Maryland,

Revenue Administration Division

o   New York – Jamie Woodward, Acting Commissioner, Department of Taxation and

Finance

o   Oregon – Ron A. Wagner, Executive Director, State Board of Tax Practitioners

➢   *5 Minute Statements*

➢   *Discussion*

Closing

Doug Shulman, Commissioner

Return Preparer Review Public Forum
September 30, 2009
10:00 – 1:00
Agenda

Welcome

Software Industry Panel   *Mark Ernst, Deputy Commissioner, Operations Support*
(Moderator)

> *Introduction of Panel Members*
>   o   Council for Electronic Revenue Communication Advancement (CERCA)-
>   Michael F. Cavanagh, Executive Director
>   o   CCH Small Firm Services – Leonard Holt, Vice President, Business
>   Development
>   o   Drake Software – John Sapp, Vice President, Sales & Marketing
>   o   Intuit, Inc. – Dan Maurer, Senior Vice President and General Manager,
>   Consumer Group

> *5 Minute Statements*

> *Discussion*

15 Minute Break

Independent Preparer Panel   *Karen L. Hawkins, Director, Office of Professional*
Responsibility   (Moderator)

> *Introduction of Panel Members*
>   o   H&R Block – Amy McAnarney, Executive Director, The Tax Institute
>   o   H&R Block Franchisee – Antonio (Tony) Zabaneh
>   o   Jackson Hewitt Franchisee – Marianne Moe
>   o   Empire Accounting & Tax Service – Cynthia MacIntosh
>   o   Independent Preparer - Raymond W. Heinen

> *5 Minute Statements*

> *Discussion*

Closing   *Mark Ernst/Karen L. Hawkins*

APPENDIX I

Competency Examination Content

Wage & NonBusiness Income Form 1040 Examination

FORMS		INCOME
1040EZ	8606	Cash
1040A	8812	
1040A Schedules 1, 2 and 3	8821 Tax Information Authorization	W-2
1040	8859 DC First Time Home Buyers Credit	W2G
1040 Schedules A, B, C-EZ, D, D-1, EIC, L, M, R, SE	8863	1098
2106EZ	8867	1098E Student Loan Interest
2120	8879	1098T
2441	8880	1099B
2555EZ	8888 Direct Deposit Voucher	1099C
3903	8889	1099DIV
4137 Unreported Tip Income	8917	1099G
4868 Extension of Time to File	9465 Request for an Installment Agreement	1099INT
5405 First Time Home Buyers Credit	1040ES	1099 MISC (box 9)
8283	1040X	1099 OID
8332	1040V	1099 R
8379 Injured Spouse	W-4/W-4P/W-4V	
8453	W-7	

Wage & Small Business Income Examination

ALL ITEMS FROM WAGE AND NONBUSINESS INCOME EXAMINATION

FORMS		
1040NR	4835	8862
1040PR	4952	8885
1040 Schedules C, D and F	5329	8903
1116	6198	8910
2106	6251	8919
2210	6252	
2439	8283	**INCOME**
2555	8396	1041 K-1
3800	8582	1065 K-1
4136	8801	1099A
4562	8814	1120S K-1
4684	8824	
4797	8839	

www.ingramcontent.com/pod-product-compliance
Lightning Source LLC
Chambersburg PA
CBHW081301180526
45170CB00007B/2517